# SHINING LIGHT

## INTO THE

# DARKNESS

*Finding God's Purposes and
Hope When Life's Events Make No Sense*

## MARK BARRETT

ISBN 978-1-63903-745-2 (paperback)
ISBN 978-1-63903-746-9 (digital)

Christian Faith Publishing
832 Park Avenue
Meadville, PA 16335
www.christianfaithpublishing.com

Printed in the United States of America

I would like to dedicate this book, first and foremost, to my wife, Barbara, who has been such a wonderful and godly partner who has supported me in writing this book, and who has walked with me through our grief. Secondly, I wish to dedicate this book to every parent and every person who has experienced a traumatic or life-altering experience that they can't explain in human terms. May this book help each one to see life through an eternal perspective from God's point of view.

# CONTENTS

# FOREWORD

Jesus reminded His followers that in this fallen world we will know suffering. But, when that suffering includes the death of a child who has known and loved the Lord, there are questions. With striking insights from Barbara, Mark provides a window into their journey with God as they come to terms with losing their son Nathan to suicide. Chapter by chapter, the reader, like the author, is thoroughly immersed in the Word of God. With freshness, we behold the enduring love of God for His children in all the circumstances of life and death. A much-needed floodlight shines on our enemy, a sometimes forgotten reality. This will be a wakeup call for many believers. To the heart of the matter, we can trust and hope in God because He is working all things together for good for those who love Him. The book while pastoral in approach is prophetic in its call for Christians to serve the Lord.

—Harry G Gardner, DMin, Consultant to the
President, Development President Emeritus Acadia
Divinity College, Wolfville, NS, Canada

In *Shining the Light into the Darkness*, Pastor Mark Barrett speaks to our deepest pain with God's deepest comfort. The book is candid and compassionate—Mark and Barbara write with honest and tender hearts to tell their story and reveal their struggle with their son's, Nathan, death. At the same time, the book is also constructive—it helps us rebuild our broken worlds upon the solid foundation of God's Word.

—Dr. Rick Reed, President—Heritage
Seminary, Cambridge, ON, Canada

Born out of the pain of suicide, *Shining Light into Darkness* offers hope to those who struggle to find meaning in life's deepest tragedies. Guided by the wisdom of years of pastoral ministry and marked by an enduring confidence in God's word to help believers struggle through and flourish in life's darkest days, the Barretts provide readers not only insights from their journey through the loss of their son but also powerful resources to comfort and encourage those who have experienced such loss. My prayer is that God will use this work to comfort and encourage those who walk a similar journey.

—Dr. David Williams, Executive Partner, Kairos University, President, Taylor Seminary, Professor of Theology and Ethics

# ACKNOWLEDGMENTS

This book has been written through tears and sorrow, with the desire that it may be an encouragement to others who have gone through some tragedy or difficulty in their life that they simply cannot explain in any way "but God." However, I believe it may be a good resource book for those who wish to counsel or encourage someone who has gone through a hardship. And finally, I believe it is a must-read book for any follower of Christ who wishes to prepare for what inevitably will come, as the Scriptures tell us that every Christian will experience trouble.

First and foremost, I wish to give thanks to my Lord for guiding me in this process of writing. John 15:5 says that as His children, we can do nothing apart of Him, and I truly believe that God gave me the inspiration, the desire, and the strength to write this book.

Second, I want to give thanks to my wife who has encouraged me in this process, who has contributed to this work in a way that gives it a more personal touch and real-life illustrations, who read through my manuscript and helped me with many details, and who has walked with me through a difficult journey. I am so grateful for Barb's support and encouragement.

Finally, I am grateful that Christian Faith Publishing took me on as a client and have edited this manuscript and given me advice on this journey as a new author. CFP has been a fantastic partner, and I am so thankful to have had the opportunity to work with this company.

# INTRODUCTION

Our life on this earth is never fair, never seems to give us the benefit of the doubt, never allows us to simply settle down and relax, and is full of surprises at every turn, surprises that are not always welcome. Isn't that the way it seems to a lot of us, especially those of us who have been through major trauma? We didn't ask for it. We don't think we did anything to deserve it. We didn't live in such a way so as to bring it on ourselves, but the trauma came nonetheless.

I grew up in a Christian home. My parents were loving, good providers, and more importantly, they wanted to point us, boys—me and two older brothers—to the Lord. Therefore, we were at church every Sunday. We attended Sunday school and church service in the morning and in the evening. I liked church. I never remember feeling as if I didn't want to go to church. I liked my Sunday school teachers, the ones I can remember. Oh, and there was Vacation Bible School too. I really liked VBS. It was fun and exciting with crafts and singing and games and an interesting Bible story told with flannel graphs. For those too young to remember flannel graphs, while telling a Bible story the teacher would use little people figures and objects cut out of colored flannel, and they would stick them on a flannel board to show the story in 3D. There was a real art in telling a story with flannel graphs, and my teachers had the knack. Two sisters who were missionaries would come to our little town of Oakhurst, California, with their trailer house and put on a week of VBS in our little country church. They loved us, kids, and we loved them. They gave us little New Testament Bibles, which I still have and I treasure all these fifty-eight years later. For many years later, these two lovely ladies sent all their VBS students birthday postcards with a handwritten note on them, in writing so small you would have to squint to read them but also had a wonderful gospel message in it. These were great and godly influences in our lives that pointed us to Jesus so that at the age of six I accepted Jesus into my heart and was immersed in the waters of believer's baptism shortly after. My point is to paint for you a picture of a life that has been lived for and filled with the things of God at the center.

My dad was a Christian businessman who was saved later in life after WWII. God made such a drastic transformation in his life that he became a strong soldier in God's army. He was often away on weekends speaking at various events, sharing his personal testimony and witnessing to the saving work of Jesus Christ. However, he also spoke of God's love to us, his family, on a regular basis. We often gathered as a family to pray together, and Dad would read the Bible and lead us in a discussion. These were always powerful times for me to be involved in as a child. My dad would pray long, passionate prayers, and as a child, I'd often wonder how he could pray so long. I'd sometimes be bored, but it made a huge impression on my life.

After my biblical education years, I entered into full-time ministry in 1982. I met my wife in a little church in Northern New Brunswick, Canada, and we were married in 1983. God gave us three beautiful boys as a gift to us from above.

We were thrilled with our family of boys, and we worked hard at showing them our love, but mostly the love of Christ. As a pastor, it would have been easy for us to tell our children that we all go to church "because your dad is the pastor." However, that's not what we wanted the boys to believe about why we go to church. We wanted to instill in their hearts that we were going to church because we love God and want to honor and worship Him. We wanted our kids to fall in love with Jesus and not just "go to church." They attended our children's program at church and memorized Scripture verses. They attended Vacation Bible Schools and missions conferences and Christian concerts. We gave them every opportunity to be exposed to Christ and the gospel, and as a result, each of them received Christ as their Savior at a very young age. Our youngest boy, Nathan, was led to Christ by his brother in their bedroom one night before going to sleep. How awesome is that?

We had a pretty typical home life with the boys. Barbara home-schooled the boys for several years. We went camping in the summers and slid down snow-packed hills on tire inner tubes in the winter. Those were challenging years of raising boys, but they were also really great days in our lives.

Nathan was a big baby at birth—ten pounds. Even so, the nurses thought he showed signs of being born premature, so they promptly put him in an incubator. He was so big he really looked funny in that enclosed crib. He almost touched both ends of the crib. The doctor was very angry when he came in and realized what had happened and that Barbara hadn't had the opportunity to hold him or to nurse him for an entire day.

As Nathan grew, although a healthy normal child, it seemed like he was slow at everything. He didn't walk until he was almost eighteen months old. His legs were so long that they hung to Barb's knees when she held him. His speech came slowly, and, as it turned out, he was never a big talker. It was often a struggle to draw a deeper conversation out of him. He just never felt the need to tell us everything in his mind, and we accepted that about him. He was the most introverted of the three boys, taking more of the personality of his mother than of me.

Nathan eventually attended a two-year Bible college and seemed to really flourish as a Christian and grow in his faith. It seemed that he was learning more and more about his own strengths and weaknesses and was beginning to figure out where God might want to use him in life. He grew up attending Christian camps and eventually volunteering his summers to work in one, and he loved every minute of it. He told us that he wanted to be in the ministry as a camp director, but then later, after Bible school, he decided that he didn't have the management skills to be a director and that he really enjoyed the maintenance side of things. To build his skill set, he decided he needed to get a trade, and he found a job working for a cabinetmaker and became an apprentice. He loved his job, and his employer loved him and his work ethic. He worked long hours and was growing in his trade. Volunteering on the weekends at a Christian winter camp, he eventually met a young lady who would become the love of his life. She was our life-long answer to prayer. Sarah also graduated from the same two-year Bible college, grew up in a Christian family, and was serving the Lord. They had so many similar interests in life, and Nathan was totally head-over-heels in love with her. He eventually proposed marriage to Sarah, and they were planning on marriage in September 2017. We, his parents, were excited about their soon marriage—part of the excitement being that our other two boys and families were living quite a distance away, so maybe for a time, we would have Nathan and Sarah a bit closer. Sarah and Nathan began talking about working in a camping ministry as full-time missionaries, and it seemed like his path was being made clearer. It was exciting to see Nathan grow, mature, get settled in life, and to anticipate a life full of service for the Lord.

On June 30, 2017, Barbara and I took an overnight mini-vacation to Niagara Falls for a getaway. Upon returning home on July 1, I received a phone text from Sarah, Nathan's fiancée. She asked if we'd seen Nathan. I told her that we just arrived back home and that we thought he was with her at the camp where she was working for the summer. She told us that he never showed up and that she couldn't reach him. Nathan was supposed to spend the weekend at the camp, where he often volunteered, so that he could spend time with Sarah. He had set everything up for his arrival. He had told the chef of the camp about the meals he would be eating while at the camp, and he had texted with Sarah the night before until about eleven in the evening, making plans for the weekend. But he was nowhere to be found.

One month earlier, Nathan had moved into his first apartment away from home. He was setting up house for when he and Sarah were married. It was in a town about thirty minutes from our home. His soon-to-be mother- and father-in-law happened to be visiting their mother in that town, so they said they'd stop by Nathan's apartment to see if he was home. I told them that he had been very tired and that if he was sleeping it would take a freight train running through his living room to wake him up. When Nathan was over-tired, he could sleep for eighteen hours straight and never wake up. He had been that kind of tired, and we assumed he was just sleeping in. His soon-to-be father-in-law headed over to his apartment where he found Nathan's car in the driveway. He pounded on the doors with no answer and found all the windows and doors locked and secured. Again, we all assumed he was sleeping. After another hour or two, I received a phone call from Karen, Sarah's mom, who said, "I think we better call the police. I'm worried about Nathan." I had been thinking the same thing only a minute earlier. But again, nobody assumed the worse of what was about to be discovered. After the police and fire department arrived and the door was busted in, they found Nathan had taken his own life.

People will no doubt say to themselves, if not aloud, "You must have seen some signs. He must have given some indication that he wasn't doing well. He must have reached out for help, but you didn't see it." That is the natural thing to think, but the reality was that we nor his friends or fiancée never saw any indication that would cause concern. Beyond being overtired, there was no indication that he might take his own life. In fact, as we went over the timeline of the previous week, he was at our house on Wednesday doing some work on our kitchen, which he had just previously installed. He had attended our church's youth group closing at a pool party on Thursday evening. He had a good day at work on Friday. He had groceries he had just purchased in the refrigerator. He had tried to submit the rent for his apartment, but the payment device wasn't working and his landlord told him to submit it the following week. His tithe for church was in his dresser drawer, and he had asked his boss to borrow the work van for Monday so that he could come to our house and finish our kitchen. That doesn't sound like the week of a person who was intending to take his life. I suppose some might even suggest that he was cleaning things up in preparation. But I believe he was just living his life responsibly. We were totally stumped for ideas as to why he would do such a horrific thing. He did leave us a note, and yet it was so spiritually dark by nature, with so much faulty thinking on a spiritual level that we just knew that it wasn't the Nathan we knew. It was obvious that he was so overwhelmed and in such a spiritual battle that he simply could not, or was not, equipped to deal with it all.

After all was said and done, this is the conclusion that Barbara and I came to: Nathan required a lot of sleep, which he wasn't getting due to long hours of work and all of his volunteerism. Secondly, Nathan was a perfectionist. That side of him was becoming more and more evident in him. He was attempting to be perfect at his work. He wanted to be the perfect Christian and eventually the perfect husband and father. He told us one time that he was going to be the favorite uncle to his nephews, whom he loved. The final blow was that he just moved to a city that is known for its demonic spiritual warfare, a city where the suicide rate had been very high and was a great concern to the city, thus, moving out from under the spiritual protection of our home and being exposed to the full force of Satan's attacks. It was all more than Nathan could endure. We don't know all of what transpired, but it seems that he must have been overwhelmed due to being overtired, coupled with his increasing perfectionist personality. But this is just us, his parents, attempting once again to find answers. He didn't reach out for help and decided to end his life.

I didn't want to write this book because it brings up so many difficult emotions in rehearsing the day of our great loss. Barbara and I were and still are completely devastated. Immediately we began looking for Christian books that would help us deal with all our emotions, our questions, and our grief. We found that most of the books dealt with suicide on a clinical level but not on an emotional or a spiritual level. We found books that talked about how to deal with death in general but few about suicide. Those that did deal with suicide were about those who had been dealing with emotional and mental issues, things that could point to a reason for the suicide. But they didn't give us the answers we had questions to. We did attend a grief share group where we found some tips for moving forward, and this was very helpful. We went to see a talented Christian counselor who also helped us to make sense of and deal with our emotions of grief and loss. However, as we continued searching for books that might help, we found a lack of good information for the kind of grief we were dealing with.

We believe that Nathan's death was a spiritual attack. Not only was it an attack on him personally, but it was also an attack on us as a ministry family. I have been in pastoral ministry since 1982 (a long time), and we have experienced spiritual attack on many levels, but this one has been the most vicious and violent and most damaging. I confess that my immediate reaction to Nathan's death was "My ministry is over. Who will ever listen to me now?" I believe that was Satan's design. He wanted to take me out of the ministry. But why me? I'm nobody. I pastor a small-town church, I'm not influencing thousands like a large city church, and I don't have a mega-TV ministry. So why me?

It's because Satan is no respecter of persons, and he will try to take any Christian out of the game. The Bible says in 1 Peter 5:8, "Be alert and of sober mind. Your enemy the devil prowls around like a roaring lion looking for someone to devour." Notice that he is seeking "someone," anyone to devour. So why not me? Satan is trying to take you out of the game also. That's why we're to be alert and sober-minded so that we can detect what Satan is doing and so that we can resist him. It was at the point of realizing what we believe had happened that I dug in my spiritual heels and committed myself to doing everything in my power to expose the plans of our spiritual enemy, to teach people the truth, and help people to be overcomers. This has become the driving force of everything I do. So many people are under attack, and yet they don't even recognize it as a spiritual battle and they just go through life in a depressed, anxious, unhappy life because they've never learned how to resist the devil. In essence, Satan is taking them out of kingdom work through depression, a lack of self-respect, anxiety, worry, a lack of self-worth, and any number of other things that take them out of living a fulfilling life in serving Christ.

The apostle Paul faced intense attacks from our enemy that were designed to crush him. Second Corinthians 4:8–9 says, "We are afflicted in every way, but not crushed; perplexed, but not driven to despair; persecuted, but not forsaken; struck down, but not destroyed." He recognized where the pressure was coming from, and he resisted the attacks. In this book I am going to share with you lessons from Scripture that I have found helpful in facing the attacks of the enemy. These lessons have also helped me with my many questions surrounding Nathan's untimely and unexpected death. They are God's answers for when life throws you a blow that is hard to explain. I hope that they will be helpful to you in dealing with your losses, your tragedy, your grief, and your pain.

CHAPTER

# Where Is God When Things Go Wrong?

## Genesis 39:20–21

Have you ever had one of those days, or weeks, or even years when everything seems to be going wrong? You called 911, and you were put on hold. You're only forty-nine years old, and you were offered the senior's discount. You're trying to lose weight, and you gained five pounds. On a more serious note, you go to the doctor one day and discover you have cancer. Or you've been trying to have a child and you miscarry. The bills were weighing heavy on you, and you lost your job. I'm pretty sure most people reading this know what I'm talking about, and your own stories are filling your thoughts as you read. It's the scenario that you're just walking through life, minding your own business, when *wham*, you get hit in the head with a two-by-four and you think, "God, where are you? I've been serving you, I've been living for you, why have you let me down like this? I don't deserve it."

Those were my exact thoughts after Nathan took his own life. My wife and I had raised him in a Christian home. We had read to him from the Bible, prayed with him, taught him godly principles, and exemplified a godly lifestyle the best we could. He was always a gentle boy and never needed harsh discipline. He had a quiet nature, what some would call an introverted nature. This made it seem like he didn't have many needs, and if he did, he didn't express them but internalized them. He attended two years of a wonderful Bible school and was flourishing in his walk with God and the direction of his life. He had long-term plans of becoming a missionary. And then *wham*, out of nowhere the unthought-of happened. No one would have ever considered gentle Nathan could even carry out such an act. Suicide would have been the furthest thing from our minds. In fact, when the police showed up at our door and told us what happened, I told them that it was not possible for him to do such a thing. I said that he must have been murdered and wondered if they had dusted for fingerprints to see who committed this crime against him. To this day I cannot imagine the pain that led our son to take his own life.

When sudden tragedy occurs, when things happen we would have never anticipated could happen, it is easy for us to turn from God and blame Him for the bad things that occur, whether to us or in our world. We conclude, "How could a loving God ever allow such an awful thing to happen?" I certainly asked that same question when Nathan died. I didn't blame God, but I wondered how God could allow it to happen. I still struggle today with questions that relate to the "Why?" and the "Why didn't God?" However, God's Word helped me in answering these questions.

Let's be reminded of Joseph of the Old Testament. Joseph had more than his share of dark days and nights. I'm sure you remember the story of how his brothers were jealous of him because of the favoritism shown him by his father Jacob. One day Jacob sent Joseph out to the fields to check on his brothers and see if they were all right. When his brother saw him coming, they plotted against him. They took him and threw him into a pit, and then they sold him to a trading caravan headed to Egypt, and from there he was sold as a slave.

His story can be found in Genesis 39:20, which says, "Then Joseph's master took him and put him into the prison, a place where the king's prisoners were confined. And he was there in the prison." He was put into a dark, dirty dungeon with some of the roughest characters in all of Egypt, and not because he had done something wrong but because he had done something right. He wasn't there because of a bad crime, but because of a good character. In fact, for a good part of his life his tombstone could have read "Nice guys finish last." And yet through it all, he remained a nice guy. The story of

Joseph gives us some lessons about how to make it when everything goes wrong.

It is no coincidence that at the beginning of the entire story about Joseph that we read about the dream he had. The dream is found in Genesis 37. His dream was prophetical by way of a promise to Joseph, and a lesson we're going to learn from this is that when everything goes wrong, remember the promises of God.

Let's take a look at the first dream as Joseph told it, found in Genesis 37:7, "There we were, binding sheaves in the field. Then behold, my sheaf arose and also stood upright; and indeed your sheaves stood all around and bowed down to my sheaf." That was a dream about how God was going to elevate Joseph above the world's resources. The second dream is found in Genesis 37:9, "Then he dreamed still another dream and told it to his brothers, and said, 'Look, I have dreamed another dream. And this time, the sun, the moon, and the eleven stars bowed down to me.'" In this dream, God told him that he was going to be elevated above the world's rulers.

Now should he have kept these dreams to himself? Could it be that when he shared them he sounded a little boastful in his tone? We don't know for sure, but maybe. Furthermore, maybe that's why his brothers were jealous. However, the reality is that these were dreams that God had given to Joseph, and God used the immaturity of Joseph and even the way in which he shared the dreams with his family to get Joseph to the right country and in the right position so that He could fulfill these dreams.

And all the while Joseph was going through those dark days, and all the while things seemed to keep going wrong for him, in all those dark days, God was preparing Joseph and training him for his future duties. And in the back of Joseph's mind was the memory that God had promised him elevation and exaltation.

You see, when dark and dreary nights come into our lives, instead of sinking on the premises, we need to stand on the promises. If it were not for the promises of God's Word, I am not certain how Barbara and I could have endured and walked through those first dark days after Nathan's death. It felt like we had been abandoned by God. Our world had completely caved in and the ground had been taken out from under our feet and we had no strength in ourselves. But we kept turning to God's Word to find help and hope. Some days I would read the Bible and feel like I was looking at blank pages. Other days I would find a verse or a thought that would encourage and refresh me. But it was remaining in the Word, even when I didn't feel I was getting anything out of it, that gave me hope and strength to walk through the day. In my journal I would write down verses from the Scripture that would remind me that God is faithful and that He loves me and cares for me no matter what. These verses became my supply line of comfort and gave me a solid foundation to stand on when it felt like there was none.

*****

*Barbara*

Although we lost the same person, our son, Mark and I grieved very differently. Yet the common ground we both have is God's Word. I have been reminded many times over the years, but especially during this time since 2017, that "Man shall not live by bread alone, but on every word that comes from the mouth of God" (Matthew 4:4). At the time of Nathan's death, I had been a Christian for forty-six years. I received Christ as my Savior when I was nine years old. Through the years I have made it a practice to memorize Scripture. Why do I share this? Because God's Word was and is the foundation that held strong through the absolute worst storm of my life. I turned to my Bible even on those days when it might not have seemed to help, but I just needed to do it out of habit. It was midfall, and I had been reading through the Psalms, looking for encouragement yet not really having anything speak fresh to me. Then I started Psalm 40, "I waited patiently for the Lord. He turned to me and heard my cry. He lifted me out of the slimy pit, out of the mud and mire. He set my feet on a rock and gave me a firm place to stand. He put a new song in my heart a hymn of praise to our God. Many will see and fear and put their trust in the Lord." Oh, my! The blessing of those three verses! It struck me that my job was to wait patiently for the Lord and everything else was up to Him. He would turn to me, hear my cry, lift me out of the slimy pit, out of the mud and mire, set my feet on rock, giving me a firm place to stand. He would even put a new song in my heart, a hymn of praise to my God. I kept reading through the Psalms, but it was these three verses that I clung to and am still reminded of when I grow impatient with this process of healing and learning to adjust to a life I never ever thought I would have to live."

*****

I can almost hear Joseph now as he makes the pit and the prison his personal platform of praise, living in the full confidence that God's promise for him would be fulfilled. In fact, I think that if the song would have been written, Joseph would have been singing it. The words go like this: "Standing on the promises that cannot fail, When the howling storms of doubt and fear assail, by the living word of God I shall prevail, standing on the promises of God." I'll tell you from personal experience that when the days were dark and when the devil had come and said to me, "What does your future look like now, Pastor?" my response has been "My future looks as bright as the promises of God." When things go wrong, remember the promises of God.

Also, when things go wrong, rely on the providence of God. Let's think about what Joseph had to go through, and let's decide how we would feel about what he went through if we were in his shoes.

Joseph's brothers were jealous of him and abused him. He was thrown into a pit by his brothers near a town called Dothan, which was known for its pits. There was a lack of water in Dothan, so they dug pits or cisterns to collect rainwater in them. They were either hollowed out of limestone bedrock or dug into the ground and lined with plaster. Since most of Israel's rainfall is confined to three or four months of the year, these cisterns collected the rainwater and made it available during the dry season. It wasn't unusual that there wasn't any water in them during this part of the year. Joseph was thrown into one of those dry pits.

From there he was sold as a slave and taken to Egypt, and then his owner's wife lied about him trying to seduce her. It was actually the other way around, but Joseph continually rejected her advances. Therefore, Joseph's master, Potiphar, had him thrown into a dungeon where he was forgotten about.

Joseph had lost his freedom because he would not compromise his purity, and he wouldn't corrupt his integrity, and he refused to cast away his dignity. In other words, he wasn't suffering for doing wrong, but for doing what was right. Peter wrote in 1 Peter 2:20, "For what credit is it if, when you are beaten for your faults, you take it patiently? But when you do good and suffer, if you take it patiently, this is commendable before God." We tend to think that if something bad happens to a good person it's because they were doing something wrong. But in reality, it could be that something bad happened because they were doing something right. Maybe it's a bit like the story of the pastor who was coming home from a missions trip. One of the church members met him at the airport, and the pastor asked how things were going. The church member said, "I've got some bad news. While you were gone, a cyclone came through town and tore my house down." The pastor responded, "To be honest with you, I've been praying for you, and I've been concerned about the way you've been living, and I think this was God's punishment on you." The church member replied, "It blew your house down too." Let's be careful about assigning blame.

Like most people who are going through deep waters that don't have an explanation, Joseph must have experienced times of doubt and confusion during the thirteen years he was a slave and in prison. It's difficult going through trials when you're doing good and you think you should be having good times. When you live a pure life, your eating habits are well-adjusted, and you exercise, yet you still end up with heart disease, it can be confusing. When you work hard at your job and end up being laid off, it can be frustrating. When you pour your heart into a relationship and it goes sour, it can be heart-breaking. When you raise a child and pour your love into him and he takes his own life, your world is turned upside down.

*****

24

*Barbara*

Sometimes, motherhood is planned and other times not. When I was just a young girl of eight, I remember being mesmerized with a young baby who was visiting our home with her mother. The first thoughts of what I wanted for my future unfolded: I wanted to be a mother. The idea was planted and would obviously take years to happen. Many years passed, and I found myself at a crossroad in my job, as the company I worked for was being bought out. The last words my boss said to me were words of encouragement to forge on in the business world. With no hesitation, my words were "All I want to be is a wife and mother." I had also felt a call to ministry, but God had not revealed what that would look like and I had only just started dating Mark in the previous couple of months. We would be married within the year, and our boys would start arriving in two-year intervals just three and a half years later. A common thought at the time was to have two children to keep things simple. Ha! Our family somehow didn't feel complete. We had our third and final son and called him Nathan. Ironically, his name means gift. There had been some difficult things that we had been processing at the time, and to name him Nathan seemed so fitting—a gift in the midst of difficulties. Little did we know that our beautiful gift from God would yield so much pain twenty-six years later. Yet losing Nathan ushered in a new period of searching and growth that would redefine the joy that his name brings—the gift of grief.

*****

The reality is that there are going to be times when you can't make sense of sorrow. There are times when the math just doesn't add up. In fact, the hardest things in life to stand are the things we don't understand. As a pastor for nearly forty years, I've seen this so many times in people's lives. I've seen mates walk away from their marriages without warning to the other one. I've performed funerals for children who died in accidents. I've sat by the bedside of people who were dying, who just weeks before seemed to be healthy and robust.

But there is a great truth we need to remember from Joseph's life, which is that just because things don't make sense to us, that doesn't mean they don't make sense. Everything that happens makes sense to God. What is hidden from us isn't hidden from God. There are going to be times that faith is going to have to swim where reason can't even wade because we believe God knows what He is doing.

When all Joseph could see was the prison, God could see the palace. That's why Joseph could say in Genesis 50:20, "But as for you, you meant evil against me; but God meant it for good, in order to bring it about as it is this day, to save many people alive." The next time life deals you a bad hand, remember these two prison promises. These are lessons I learned the first few months after Nathan's death.

The first one comes from Romans 8:28, "And we know that all things work together for good to those who love God, to those who are the called according to His purpose." That verse is so familiar to many of us who have been followers of Christ for a long time that we often don't take it as seriously as we should. This verse came to life for me the months after our tragedy. You see, we don't always see it in the immediate. It might take God some time to bring it about. We might even grow impatient in waiting. But just like Jesus turned the water into wine, God will take something bad that has happened to us and turn it into something good. We don't have to understand the bad thing that has happened, and we don't even have to understand the promise. But what we do have to do is to believe what God has said and begin to live in the hope of our future in God. Almost immediately after Nathan's death, both Barbara and I agreed that God had to use this tragedy for good in some way. To be honest, we're still waiting for that promise to be fulfilled. We haven't seen people turn to the Lord because of it. We haven't seen any great transformation in the lives of people yet. But we believe in this promise from the Lord, and we're continuing to live our life in light of it, and we know that God will turn it into something good.

The second prison promise is found in Psalm 138:8, "The Lord will perfect that which concerns me; Your mercy, O Lord, endures forever; Do not forsake the works of Your hands." In other words, the

Lord will surely fulfill His purpose for our life, and we can rely on the providence of God to do so.

Another lesson we learn from Joseph's life is that when everything goes wrong, we can rest in the presence of God. Joseph was girded by the promises of God, he was guided by the providence of God, and he was guarded by the presence of God. Genesis 39:2 says, "The Lord was with Joseph." Verse 3 says, "His master saw that the Lord was with him." Verse 21 says, "But the Lord was with Joseph." In verse 23, we're told, "Because the Lord was with him." Every step of the way God was with Joseph. He was with Joseph when he was down in the pit. He was with him when he was a slave. And God never forgot about him when he was in prison. God was with Joseph in the same way that when Noah was in the ark, navigating his way through the storm, God was with him. In the same way that when the three Hebrew men were thrown into the fiery furnace, God got into the fire with them. In the same way that when Daniel was thrown into the lion's den, God shut the mouths of the lions because he was there with Daniel. When the disciples were in that boat on the stormy sea, Jesus got into the boat with them. And as children of God, there might be times when we feel lonely and deserted, but it's impossible for us to ever be alone. No matter how deep the water, you never drown. No matter how hot the furnace, you'll never burn because you can count on the presence of God. When Nathan died, for the first week we had lots of friends who came to visit us and comfort us. Our other two sons and wives came to be with us and to attend the funeral. But then after the funeral, everyone left, and there was just Barbara and me. The house was too quiet. After a while the phone stopped ringing, and everyone else went back to work to their own families and their own lives. We would see people in the stores, at church, or in a Bible study; and for other people life returned to normal. Rarely did anyone ask us how we were doing, how we were handling life, how they could be praying for us. It was very lonely on the people side, but we were comforted in knowing that God had never left us and that He was walking with us through the storm. We could feel His hand upon us giving us strength to handle the journey each day. The journey isn't over yet. Almost four years later we are still grieving our loss. Some days we grieve in tears, and some days there is simply a feeling of emptiness. This is the process of grief that we need to go through and should not push away and we should embrace as part of the healing process.

When it seems like everything is going wrong and there is no end in sight, we need to respond with the patience of God.

In Genesis 39:20, we are told, "Then Joseph's master took him and put him into the prison, a place where the king's prisoners were confined. And he was there in the prison." Keep in mind that Joseph was only about seventeen years old at the time. Genesis 41:46 tells us, "Joseph was thirty years old when he stood before Pharaoh king of Egypt. And Joseph went out from the presence of Pharaoh, and went throughout all the land of Egypt." Put those two verses together and you realize Joseph was in prison for thirteen years for doing what was right. He was in prison because of his jealous brothers, a lying woman, and an ungrateful butler. It's amazing to me that all during his time in prison he never got bitter, he never held a grudge, and he never took revenge. When he finally became the prime minister of Egypt, he never mentioned his brothers who sold him into slavery, he never said anything about Potiphar's wife who had seduced him and lied about him and had him thrown into prison, he never uttered a word about the butler who forgot to mention Joseph after Joseph had gotten him about of prison, but he just kept on keeping on, loving and living for God, keeping his mind and heart on God's promises.

Here's the key to Joseph's success in all that he did and to his steady mind. His commitment was dependent on an unfailing, all-knowing, ever-present God. Someone has said that you can tell the size of a Christian by what it takes to stop him. I know of so many Christians who have gone through difficult days, and they are filled with bitterness, haunted with revenge, and they shake their fist at God and say, "Is this the best You have for me? Because if it is, I don't want any part of it." Barbara and I never had those thoughts. We were and we are confident that because God is an all-knowing God, He knew infinitely what Nathan was going through, that He was there by His spirit when Nathan took his last breath but for some reason allowed it anyway. We cannot understand all the reasons, for who can know the mind of God? But we are confident that God has a plan, and we are standing on His promises. The enemy intended this for evil, but God intended it for good. Martin Luther said something that might not seem earth-shattering, but it says a lot about him. He said, "Even if I knew that tomorrow the world would go to pieces, I will still plant my little apple tree and pay my debts." What he was saying is that no matter what happens tomorrow, he was going to do what is right, be right, and live right. You see, true commitment is not conditional. If a person will not serve God in a prison, then he's not fit to serve God in a palace.

Where is God when everything or even some things go wrong? Where is He when sleep won't come? Where is He when we wake up in a hospital bed with pain that will not stop? Where is He when the unthinkable happens in our lives? Let me assure you that when you hurt, God hurts. When you are stuck in your prison, God is right there with you even as He was with Joseph. Why did Jesus weep at the tomb of Lazarus when He knew He was going to raise him from the dead? Because He weeps with us and understands our sorrows. When no one listens to you, God listens. When you wipe away tears of loneliness, or frustration, or anguish, in heaven there is a pierced hand approaching a heavenly face and wiping a tear.

Sometimes storms of life come along to teach us that God is in control and that we can lean on Him. It is those times that God is trying to draw us closer to Himself. Oh, and one more thing. There isn't anything louder than the silence of our heavenly father. Don't interpret His silence as a lack of love because we know when everything goes wrong, God is right here with us.

# God's Grace

## Romans 5:1–21

A lot of churches are not singing the great hymns of the faith anymore, but perhaps you know the hymn written by Julia H. Johnston in 1910. The hymn is a commentary of Romans 5:20b, which says, "But where sin increased, grace abounded all the more." These are the words of the first two stanza's.

Marvelous grace of our loving Lord,
Grace that exceeds our sin and our guilt!
Yonder on Calvary's mount outpoured,
There where the blood of the Lamb was spilled.

Grace, grace, God's grace,
Grace that will pardon and cleanse within;
Grace, grace, God's grace,
Grace that is greater than all our sin!

Sin and despair, like the sea waves cold,
Threaten the soul with infinite loss;
Grace that is greater, yes, grace untold,
Points to the refuge, the mighty cross.

I wonder if you believe what this hymn is communicating? If you do, on what basis do you believe it? Do you really believe that God's grace exceeds our sin and our guilt? Furthermore, what kind of sin does grace exceed? Does it exceed just some sin or all sin? What if you are a follower of Christ and you consciously make a decision to do what you know is wrong, like to take your own life, or to commit adultery, or view pornography, or cheat on your taxes? Does God's grace exceed those sins? I know that there are some theological circles who will proclaim that anyone who commits suicide will go straight to hell. On what basis have they formed this theology? And is it correct theology according to Scriptures? However, there are other sins you might be thinking about. What about lust? Does God's grace exceed lust? What about lying, and cheating, and stealing? Or what about murder? Could it be possible that God's grace can exceed murder? What about the drunk driver who runs into a person and kills them? How about envy or pride? Does God's grace exceed every sin and guilt or just some sins that we recognize as forgivable sins?

That's the question I want to deal with in this chapter. It's a question I had to deal with early on after Nathan took his life. I had to search the heart of God through the Word of God to find the answers to my question. Nathan received Christ as his Lord and Savior early in life. Actually, it was his older brother who led him to Christ. Nathan shared a bedroom with his brother, and as the story goes, one night before they went to sleep his older brother talked to him about Jesus and he accepted Him into his heart. Later, when I heard the story I sat down with Nathan to explain the gospel fully to him, as I wasn't certain as to what his older brother had communicated to him, and we confirmed the decision he had made. A few years later he was baptized. We saw very clear evidence in his life of his relationship with Christ, which are the fruit of the Spirit, and we believe that he walked with the Lord. But how could a committed Christian commit such a heinous crime against himself? Was he really saved, and did Christ admit him into His heaven? Did grace cover his sin? I needed answers to my questions in the same way that perhaps you are asking the same question about other sins that you or others around you have committed. You're wondering if your sin,

31

or the sin of others, can ever be forgiven. Of course, we believe 1 John 1:9 that tell us, "If we confess our sins, he is faithful and just to forgive us our sins and to cleanse us from all unrighteousness." But that verse is for the living. What if we die without having the chance to confess our sin? Does grace cover that sin?

In this chapter we're going to discover that God's grace, which was offered on the cross, is the same grace that is extended to us throughout our life and to every sin. The scripture I will be referring to is found in Romans 5.

Romans is a book of logic, and it's full of *therefore*s. You see, the *therefore* of condemnation in Romans 5:1, the *therefore* of justification in Romans 3:20, the *therefore* of no condemnation in Romans 8:1, and the *therefore* of dedication in Romans 12:1. However, in Romans 5 there is a larger message of salvation that I want to describe for you. It is a message that has to do with God's grace. It is what God gives to us when we accept it, but it is the one thing so many Christians miss, or misinterpret, or disregard in favor of what makes more sense to the human mind, which is simple obedience. For example, we say that we are saved by grace through faith, but then many people proceed to attempt to be saved through the good works that they do. How do I know that? I know it when people make statements like "I'm not a very good Christians because I don't do this or that or the other thing." And they name things they see others do or what they think a "good Christian" should do. That kind of statement shows me that they are trying to be a good Christian by their good works and not by faith. Or someone will say, "I wish I could be like so and so; they're a real Christian." That shows me that they think a real Christian can only look a certain way and that they have to do certain things. Another example might be that someone might say, "Maybe I'm not saved because I keep sinning." That shows me that they are basing their faith on their human ability to sin or not to sin and that maybe a Christian should achieve sinless perfection. It shows me that they really have not laid claim to God's grace in its fullest sense because they still believe they aren't worthy to be saved.

In one sense they are right, in that none of us are worthy to be saved. But they are wrong in that God didn't save any of us because we are worthy, but because we aren't worthy and we will never be worthy. Christ didn't come into this world to find good people who could fend for themselves and who didn't need a Savior. Jesus came into this world to look for sinners, for sick people, for people who couldn't do anything to save themselves, people who didn't deserve salvation, people who couldn't fend for themselves and who knew that if it weren't for Jesus, they would die in their sin, the scum of the world, people no one else would even look at. Jesus came for people like me and you.

In order for us to fully understand this concept, we must define grace. In an objective sense, grace is the receiving of something or anything that brings favor or pleasure. For example, grace was given to me when God led my wife, Barbara, into my life. She brings me great pleasure on so many different levels. Or to a lesser degree, it is pure grace when you eat your favorite ice cream, or dessert, or meal. Eating them can bring great pleasure. However, when we apply grace in the spiritual realm, it is something that has been redefined by God. Grace really was not a concept that was known in the Old Testament era of the law. In many ways, the law was black-and-white. Do this; don't do that. It was pretty simple. It was designed to show man how sinful he was. But God took grace to a new level in the New Testament through Jesus Christ. When Jesus died on the cross for our sins, He offered the grace gift of forgiveness. It was given freely, with no expectation of return, with its only motive being found in the abundance and free-heartedness of the giver.

Now grace always comes before mercy. As theologians define it, mercy is not getting what we deserve because what we deserve is to be punished for our sins. Then grace came along and offered us something we don't deserve, which is the free gift of eternal life. God offers this grace gift through His Son, Jesus Christ. Once we accept His offering, He gives the mercy we require.

Who can have this grace? It's tempting to think that only *good* people deserve grace. But the Bible says in Romans 10:13, "For everyone who calls on the name of the Lord will be saved." God doesn't withhold His grace from one person because their sin is greater than another person. In fact, He doesn't withhold His grace from anyone who will call on His name to be saved. You might ask, "What about the rapist, or the mass murderer, or the thief, or career criminal? Can they be saved?" The answer is that *whoever* calls on the name of the Lord will be saved. Aren't you glad that grace doesn't withhold its love from anyone? Otherwise, none of us could be saved. One person's sin is no greater than another person's sin because grace is greater than any sin.

This truth has greatly encouraged me over the years when I think of Nathan and his sin. I can't even imagine the pain he must have been in and what it was that caused such pain that he would take his own life. Yet he was one who had called on the name of the Lord and truly believed that Christ is the Savior for sin. Notice that Romans 10:13 says that the person who calls on the name of the Lord "will be saved." Salvation isn't conditional on how good we can be, or on how many days we can go without sinning, or on any other good deed we can perform, but its only condition is Christ's ability to save the one who calls on His name. In addition, we are given reassurance in Hebrews 7:25 where it says, "Consequently, he is able to save to the uttermost those who draw near to God through him, since he always lives to make intercession for them." What man's effort cannot achieve, Christ's finished work on the cross has already done. The words "to the uttermost" are powerful words. They are the same words found in Luke 13:11 in describing the plight of the crippled woman. She had a condition that caused her to be bent over so that she couldn't straighten her back completely. The description of her condition is described using the same Greek words. However, Christ does save completely because His sacrifice on the cross was the perfect sacrifice with no limitations. Christ saves us entirely and forever. This truth in no way gives us permission to sin, but when we do sin, we know that grace is greater than all our sins.

If you are wondering what you need to do to obtain this wonderful gift of grace, you don't have to do anything. It is a gift given to us entirely through faith. Romans 5:1–2 says, "Therefore, since we have been justified by faith, we have peace with God through our Lord Jesus Christ. Through him we have also obtained access by faith into this grace in which we stand, and we rejoice in hope of the glory of God." Look at what we gain by faith. First, we are justified by faith. To be justified means to free a man from his guilt, which stands in the way of his being right with God or with the law. When a person receives a speeding ticket, they can either just pay the fine, or they can stand before a judge to argue their case and then possibly pay a reduced fine. In either case, after the fine is paid they are released from the guilt of not being right with the law. In the same way when we talk about having a right relationship with God, it is our sin of unbelief that condemns us before God. John 16:8–9 says, "And when he comes, he will convict the world concerning sin and righteousness and judgment: concerning sin because they do not believe in me." Judgment for the sin of unbelief will always result in eternal separation from God. However, Jesus stepped up and paid the penalty for our sin when He died on the cross, and as a result we get set free from the penalty of our sin at the moment we place our faith in Jesus Christ and in what He did for us.

What is faith? Faith is a firm persuasion or conviction based on hearing the truth about the message of salvation. Our faith cannot be based on what we can do to save ourselves because the Bible says in Ephesians 2:1, "And you were dead in the trespasses and sins." This is talking about being dead to spiritual things. People who are dead to spiritual things can't do anything to rescue themselves. Their deliverance has to come from an outside source. And that's why the apostle Paul wrote in Galatians 1:3–4, "Grace to you and peace from God our Father and the Lord Jesus Christ, who gave himself for our sins to deliver us from the present evil age, according to the will of our God and Father."

When I read that verse, I think of the incident of when I was very young, perhaps seven or eight years old. I have two older brothers, and our parents had taken us to Bass Lake in Southern California for a time of fun in the water. On that day, our parents rented a kayak for us to play in. My older brother and I got into the boat and began paddling. Well, you can only imagine that at that age I didn't do a very good job at paddling, which frustrated my older brother to no end. In attempting to show me how to paddle, we flipped the kayak. I'm not sure of the distance we were from shore, but at that age it felt like a mile. Oh, and one other problem. We didn't have life preservers on. Those were the days when you didn't worry about that sort of thing. There were no seatbelts in cars either. Even if there were, you didn't use them and they got lost somewhere in the crack of the seat. We rode in the back of pickup trucks and thought it was a good time. So we had no life preservers on. In addition, I owned a pair of cowboy boots that I adored and wore everywhere. On this occasion, I had my cowboy boots on in the kayak when it flipped. Now I knew how to swim, but I had cowboy boots on. I felt like I was making progress as I attempted to swim toward shore, but I had cowboy boots on. We must have been out of sight of our parents, but a man on the beach observed what was going on and thankfully he swam out to rescue me. He dragged the kayak to shore, took my boots off, put life preservers on us, placed my boots in the boat beside me, and away we went again. The point is that my rescue that day came from an outside force. I'm pretty certain that if that man had not been available to rescue me that day, most likely I would have drowned.

There was a day in my life, and perhaps in your life, when I was persuaded that what Jesus did for me on the cross was all that needed to be done to make me right before God. Our justification isn't given to us because we can somehow make ourselves good enough, or clean enough, or right enough, any more than I could have saved myself wearing my cowboy boots in the lake that day. I couldn't have saved myself through having right thoughts, by dreaming of dry land, by imagining that I could float indefinitely, or by any other means except an outside source of help. So it is by faith alone that we believe Jesus did everything that needed to be done to pay for our justification, and we simply put our faith in His promise to save us. As a result, we have peace with God by faith. Romans 5:1 says, "Therefore, since we have been justified by faith, we have peace with God through our Lord Jesus Christ." To have peace means to live in a state of untroubled, undisturbed well-being. All of us would have to admit that there are times when there is an inconsistency in our walk with God. Sometimes we live in light of His Word and do things that please Him, but not always. Sometimes we let anger have the upper hand. Sometimes we let our minds wander, and we don't think the thoughts we ought to be thinking. Sometimes we don't treat people with love, and sometimes we say no when we should say yes and we say yes when we should say no.

Now if we were justified by works, then we should have peace with God as long as we're doing good things. However, if we fail in doing good, then that peace would be broken. However, having peace with God means that even when we're doing something wrong, we still have faith in Jesus Christ. Our belief in Him hasn't changed. Therefore, because our peace with God is squarely founded on justification by faith, we can always have peace with God. Psalm 32:2 (NKJV) says, "Blessed is [or how happy is] the man to whom the Lord does not impute iniquity." The word *impute* means to credit to one's account or to charge one with. When you go to the store and buy a beautiful new outfit, and you go to the cashier and use your credit card, the store *imputes* the cost of the outfit to your account. You are charged with the amount of the outfit, and you are required to pay it. However, God has already *imputed* the cost of our sin to Jesus, and He paid for it on the cross. Therefore, when we put our trust in Him, sin is no longer imputed on us and we have peace with God.

Also, we give access to grace by faith. Romans 5:2a (ESV) says, "Through him we have also obtained access by faith into this grace in which we stand." God doesn't owe us anything. We need to get away from the idea that we have to give God a reason to show us His grace or that in some way we have to show God that we deserve His grace. It's not like when I was attempting to win the attention and love of the girl I eventually married by doing kind things for her, by opening the car door for her, by sending her roses, and by saying complimentary things to her. I hope those aren't the reasons alone that Barbara eventually fell in love with me, but maybe they helped the process along. But that's not the way it works to win God's grace. God doesn't require us to clean up our act, improve our life, and show Him that we are worthy before He gives us His grace. On the contrary, God loves us so much that it is out of His nature of love that He gives us this undeserved blessing of grace. Romans 5:8(ESV) says, "But God shows his love for us in that while we were still sinners, Christ died for us."

This wonderful grace is given to us as a gift from God through faith. Romans 5:15 continues, "But the free gift is not like the trespass. For if many died through one man's trespass, much more have the grace of God and the free gift by the grace of that one man Jesus Christ abounded for many." Simply put, grace is given to us as a gift from God's Son. Let me try to break that verse down for you. The word *but* brings out the contrast between Adam and Christ. First comes the negative when the verse says "the free gift is not like the trespass." Adam's *trespass* brought death to all men. Many wonder how that is faith. Why do we have to suffer today because of Adam's sin? Perhaps it might help if I ask you if it is fate that you got your mother's freckles or your dad's nose? You see, we inherited certain features from our parents, whether we like it or not. In the same way, we inherited Adam's sin nature. We're not a sinner because we sin. We sin because we are a sinner.

Here's the good news. God's gift brought life to all who will accept it. In other words, grace is more powerful than sin. Notice the expression in verse 15, "the free gift." A gift isn't a gift unless it is truly free. Although justification and salvation are free, they aren't cheap. They were purchased at an infinite cost, the cost of Jesus dying on Calvary's tree. The greatest display of God's grace toward us is found in the gift of Jesus Christ, God's only begotten Son. Later in the book of Romans, Paul will write in 8:32, "He who did not spare his own Son but gave him up for us all, how will he not also with him graciously give us all things?" Is grace greater than all our sin? Give me a resounding *yes*!

As further encouragement, let's see what God's grace does for us. Romans 5:20 states, "Now the law came in to increase the trespass, but where sin increased, grace abounded all the more." In other words, grace allows us to reign in life. The law that God gave to Moses on Mt. Sinai wasn't given so that if we could or would somehow obey it, we would become more spiritual. There are some who believe that to be true. But the opposite is true. The word *abound* means to bring it out in the open. It's like when I'm studying my

Bible or when I'm reading a book, I read with a pen or a highlighter in my hand. When I come to something I want to go back to and remember or study in greater detail, I will underline or highlight that sentence, or I will write down the thought. Then when I go back to it, my eye is easily attracted to that sentence. In the same way, God's standard of perfection is so important that He brought the law through Moses so that our transgressions would become more obvious or highlighted. You see, the law served to highlight our need for grace. That's why legalistic teaching of the Word of God never decreases sin, but it increases it. The more we try to be righteous by obeying the law perfectly, the more we realize we can never do it. And although we know that to be true, sometimes we'll get on the performance treadmill and try to work, work, work with the goal of somehow winning the love of God. In doing so, we paralyze ourselves with legalistic expectations of ourselves that God never put on us.

I sometimes wonder if this is what happened in the mind of our son, Nathan. He tended to be a perfectionist, and we know from reading his journals and other tidbits we've picked up along the way that he was striving to be the perfect Christian, the unfailing worker, the best uncle, and the ideal husband. He readily would assist anyone who needed his help and tirelessly offered his services "as unto God." In fact, he ran himself so hard that he was exhausted the week of his suicide. Not only was he helping with a Christian camp on the weekends, but he also served in the church youth ministry, he was helping us to install a new kitchen in our home (he was a cabinetmaker by trade), he was helping friends with odd jobs along the way, and he was intensely involved in planning his wedding. All of those looked like good things on the surface, but one can't help but wonder if he somehow felt that this was his way of earning grace. Did he have it in his mind that unless he did all these things perfectly, somehow he would not be accepted? And perhaps if he didn't get it all right, then maybe he wasn't saved at all. From what we have been able to read between the lines, this scenario seems likely. Now to the degree of sounding like a protective father and trying to make things better than what they are, I believe that Nathan had accepted Christ as Savior and Lord and that he truly believed he was saved by grace alone. Not for one minute do I believe he was trying to work his way to salvation, but I do wonder if he missed the wonder of grace as so many of us do.

Let's look further into this marvelous grace. Romans 5:20b says, "But where sin increased, grace abounded all the more." You see, grace wasn't an addition to God's plan, but it was a part of His plan from the beginning. God dealt with Adam and Eve in grace by removing them from the garden. He dealt with the patriarchs in grace when they messed up and deserved punishment. He dealt with the nation of Israel in grace when He deported them for their sins. He didn't give the law to Moses to replace grace, but to show us our need for grace. The law was temporary, but grace is eternal.

Furthermore, God's grace is more than adequate to deal with all our sin. Remember at the beginning of this section that sin and death were reigning? And now at the end, grace is reigning. The phrase translated "abounded all the more" literally means "super-abounded." It's like the day Barbara and I walked in a Purdy's Candy Shop. We didn't intend on buying anything (yeah, right!), but we were just looking around and the saleslady approached us and asked us if we like Turtles. Not the animal kind of turtle, but the chocolate kind with caramel and pecans encrusted with a chocolate coating. We said, "Yes, we do." She asked us if we had ever tried Purdy's Turtles. (They call them *Sweet Georgia Browns*.) She proceeded to describe them as Turtles on steroids. And believe me, they are just how she described them. When Paul was describing God's grace, it's the same kind of idea as Purdy's Sweet Georgia Browns. He's describing grace on steroids. He's describing super-abounding grace. It's a description of something that is growing out of measure, beyond proportion, and out of its banks to a far-stretched extreme. In 2017 the United States experienced the effects of Hurricane Irma. It was one of the most powerful Atlantic hurricanes in recorded history. It was a category 5 storm with winds 185 miles per hour for thirty-seven hours. It held seven trillion watts of energy, twice as much as all bombs used in World War II. Do you get the picture? The waters rose higher than the rivers and water systems could handle, and it overflowed and flooded the towns and cities. This is a picture of the marvelous grace Paul was talking about. Romans 5:20 could be written like this: "For wherever sin exists in abundance and is multiplying and constantly expanding, that is precisely the time and place where grace is poured out in a far greater, surpassing quantity."

Let me tell you that regardless of where we live or what circumstance we're facing and regardless of how bad the situation around us looks to our natural eyes, the grace of God is flowing downstream like Hurricane Irma, and God is pouring out His grace in abundant measure. In fact, it's impossible for us to imagine, measure, or even dream of the amount of divine grace God is sending in our direction. No banks can hold the flood of grace He's sending our way. It isn't just a lot of grace, but it is more, and more, and more, and much more grace. The flood of grace will always far surpass the flood of sin and darkness.

I felt like Nathan's death was the end of my ministry. I wondered who would even be interested in hearing me preach after this. But that is a lie from the devil whose only goal is to keep us from being light and salt in this world and keep us from doing the will of God. But never forget that the enemy cannot prevail against us if we will yield to the Lord. If we surrender to His divine grace, it will rise higher and higher until it eventually floods every area of our lives. So instead of seeing the destruction of the enemy, we will see the awesome outpouring of the marvelous grace of God everywhere we look. And let me add that it is important to look for His grace. It isn't always apparent, but it is always there. The only time I can't see God's grace is when I allow myself to get so deep into the hole of my own self-pity, grief, and pain that it overshadows God's grace. That has happened for sure. But when I lift my eyes off my own pain, it's then that I see the wonders of God's grace being exposed, sometimes in the most unlikely places and ways.

*****

## *Barbara*

As much as the early days for Mark and me were spent in study and grieving side by side, I was in a state of quiet shock yet trying to come to grips with the reality of the turn in our lives that we never imagined. As Mark has said, he thought his ministry was over. In the time that I was able to be involved in ministry, I had worked predominately with women, young women, women raising children. The question I had was, "Why would anyone ever listen to anything I had to say again?" It was with this question that God showed how His grace extended to myself as well. As much as I had not served out of a need to earn my salvation but simply out of a love to serve, God showed me the cracks in my thinking. Are we only of use in His kingdom if we always have everything turn out okay in the eyes of ourselves and those around us? I knew before Nathan died that I was not perfect and still had so much to learn. One of my life verses is Philippians 1:6, "Being confident of this, that he who began a good work in you will carry it on to completion until the day of Christ Jesus." I believe that as humans we navigate to measuring everything visually even if we are not seeking to do that. If I wasn't perfect before Nathan died and was able to serve faithfully, why should my service be affected afterward? Well, I had faulty thinking and didn't realize it. My faithfulness in service does not mean that I will necessarily see what I think I should see. In the great faith chapter of Hebrews 11, verse 39 says, "These were all commended for their faith, yet none of them received what had been promised."

At this moment, it has been three years, seven months, and sixteen days of a journey of grace with God. He has given me the time and space to be with Him in a way that I never had before. Eighteen months before Nathan died, the Lord led Mark and I to the decision that I would step back from part-time employment so that I could focus on women's ministry. I did just that, but when Nathan died, I needed to step back from this as well. I was gifted time that few have to deal with the trauma of the shock of loss and all the additional losses that come with losing a child. I had time to adapt to life with sleepless nights and a repeat of the words I heard over and over again in my head, that my life had changed forever. I had time to seek counseling and then time to recover from all that it took out of me. Most importantly, I had time to spend, just spend with God. I had begun prayer journaling in my early thirties and had been pretty faithful with it. Now it was a lifeline as it seemed to be the only way I could pour out my heart and my anguish to God. The pen in hand slowed my thoughts down and unravelled the mess of knots in my head. Yes, I call this the grace of God too. He has walked me through each and every step of each and every day.

*****

The next time you think your situation looks bad, don't be too surprised when you sense God telling you in your spirit to keep pressing on, "Don't give up! Pour it on! Keep it up! Don't stop for a minute! Keep pressing ahead! It's in dark and difficult moments like these that I love to work the most! This is when my grace super-exceeds the darkness of the world." Whenever sin and darkness are present, this is when God pours out His grace.

It is the marvelous grace of God that has inspired the writings of many through the ages. Newton was involved in the slave trade when he came to the realization of what a horrible sinner he was and sought the forgiveness of God. As a result of the grace he found, he wrote the beloved words we sing, "Amazing grace, how sweet the sound, that saved a wretch like me. I once was lost, but now I'm found, was blind but now I see." Charles Wesley wrote the words in his song, "And can it be that I should gain an interest in the Savior's blood, died He for me, who caused His pain?" Haldor Lellenas wrote these wonderful words: "Wonderful grace of Jesus, taking away my sin, how shall my tongue describe it, where shall its praise begin, taking away my burden, setting my spirit free, for the wonderful grace of Jesus reaches me." And Julia Johnstone penned the words "Dark is the stain that we cannot hide; What can we do to wash it away? Look! There is flowing a crimson tide, brighter than snow you may be today. Marvelous, infinite, matchless grace, freely bestowed on all who believe! You that are longing to see His face, will you this moment His grace receive?"

I believe that because of God's wonderful grace that is greater than all our sin, I will one day see our son Nathan again in heaven. He may have doubted himself. He may have struggled with the weakness of his own sinful nature. He made a horrible decision to escape his weakness and pain through suicide, but God's grace is greater than all our sin and is able to deliver us, even through our sin.

CHAPTER

# Saved, Saved, Saved

## John 10:27–29

My motivation for writing this chapter is to encourage those who have lost loved ones by suicide, those who once claimed Christ to be their Savior from sin and eternal punishment. But maybe it's not suicide. Maybe there is a fear for a loved one who has been caught in the snare of a sinful habit, or they've begun running with the wrong crowd, or have begun questioning their belief system. Is that person, who once claimed Christ as their Savior, saved for eternity? Just because a person says they are a Christian doesn't always mean they really are. Suicide complicates everything, and one of the things that brought turmoil to my heart was in wondering whether or not Nathan was truly saved. Once again, this led me to God's Word where we find all the answers.

What do you think of when you hear the word *secure*? Maybe you think of the locks on the doors of your house, and when you go to bed at night you go around and lock all your doors so that your family can be secure. One day we got a phone call from our son Evan, who told us that the night before he woke up in the middle of the night sensing that someone was in their bedroom. Evan wears glasses, and his sight is quite limited without them. However, when he looked at the door of his bedroom, he could see a figure standing there. This man had entered their home through their back door, and he was in their bedroom. I don't know if Evan was brave or foolish, but I admire that he got up and started yelling at the guy to get out of his house and he chased him out the front door and called the police. Guess what he did next? He called a security company and had a security system installed on his doors. Months after that, Barb and I were visiting them and staying at their house. One night everyone had gone to bed, and I was the last one up. I thought I heard their cat meowing at the back door. They usually bring her in at night, but I thought I heard her, so I opened the back door to take a look and their alarm went off in the house. It almost gave me heart failure as I realized what I had done. But I discovered that their house was secure.

For you, maybe you think of a prison, where people who have committed crimes are locked behind iron doors and barbed wire fences. They have been securely put away for a crime they have committed. Or maybe you think of a bank where you keep your money. In your mind, at least, your money is safe and secure where no one can steal it. It used to be that people would hide their money under a mattress or dig a hole in the backyard and hide it in a tin can. Nowadays, we put our money in banks for security.

If you have submitted your life to the Lord as your Savior, is your salvation secure? Perhaps there was a day when you entrusted your soul to the Savior, Jesus Christ, and you said you wanted to know His salvation in hopes of living with Him for eternity. But is your soul indeed secure? Was the salvation of our son Nathan secure? Is it possible to fall too far away from the path of following Jesus Christ that you are no longer saved? Is it possible to commit such a vile act of sin that God will turn His back on you and say, "I'm taking my salvation back. I don't want to be your heavenly father any more?"

This is a question and a deep theological truth that people are missing in their understanding today. Maybe they never understood it in the first place. As much as I have studied this topic over the years, I still had to review it again to make sure I understood it and to be sure in my heart that Nathan's salvation is secure. You see, this is a truth that, if we miss it, can lead us to live a hopeless life.

In this chapter I am going to share with you why God says that if you are a saved person, you can never, ever be a lost soul again.

The first reason is that nothing can separate us from the love of God, which is in Christ Jesus our Lord. As you read Romans 8:38–39, see if you can find anything left out of these sentences that might separate us from the love of Jesus. "For I am sure that neither death nor life, nor angels nor rulers, nor things present nor things to come, nor powers, nor height nor depth, nor anything else in all creation, will be able to separate us from the love of God in Christ Jesus our Lord."

"For I am sure that neither death nor life." That pretty much covers everything already. The apostle Paul says that I am persuaded that anything that happens—not death, or anything that happens after death, or anything that happens while you are living—can separate you from the love of God.

"nor angels"—Good or bad angels. The devil is a fallen angel.

"nor rulers"—That is referring to kingdoms.

"nor powers"—That is referring to authorities in those kingdoms.

"nor things present"—That means anything in this present life we live in.

"nor things to come"—Anything that might be created in the future.

"nor height"—That is talking about anything in the heavens.

"nor depth"—That is anything in hell

And in case he left anything out, he adds, "Nor anything else in all creation, will be able to separate us from the love of God in Christ Jesus our Lord."

If there is any one verse in the entire Bible that deals with our security in Christ, this one covers all the bases. It tells us that there is absolutely nothing that can separate a child of God from the love of the Lord. Now of course we are talking about a person who is genuinely saved. Not everyone who professes to be saved is actually saved. But you knew that, right? Listen to what Jesus says in Matthew 7:22–23, "On that day many will say to me, 'Lord, Lord, did we not prophesy in your name, and cast out demons in your name, and do many mighty works in your name?' And then will I declare to them, 'I never knew you; depart from me, you workers of lawlessness.'" It appears that outwardly these people looked like they were saved. They seemed to be doing what looks like someone who is saved should do. But Jesus declared they were never truly saved. They didn't lose their salvation, but they never had salvation to begin with. There is a difference between those who know and those who never knew. Those who Jesus never knew didn't lose their salvation. They may have been religious. They tried to do some good works. They even went to church on a regular basis. But they never entered into a personal relationship with Jesus Christ by faith.

Perhaps you have heard someone make the statement that "I know someone who was once saved, but now they're lost." I would say to that person, "No, you don't. You know someone who you thought was saved but was really lost." I can say that because according to the Scriptures a person who was truly saved can never, ever be lost.

Someone else might comment, "What about those people who were pastors, deacons, and leaders in the church, but now they turned away from God and they're living in sin and some are atheists?" The Bible says that they were never saved in the first place. First John 2:19 tells us, "They went out from us, but they were not of us; for if they had been of us, they would have continued with us. But they went out, that it might become plain that they all are not of us." There is a saying that goes, "The faith that fizzles at the finish had a flaw from the first." These people were never truly saved from the first, and we know it because nothing can separate us from the love of God and God's children will continue in their faith no matter what.

Second, a saved person can never be lost again because we're made perfect forever. Now stay with me. I am not speaking of sinless perfection while we're living on earth. Hebrews 10:14 says, "For by a single offering he has perfected for all time those who are being sanctified." The word *sanctified* is referring to those who are saved. When Jesus died on the cross, He died one time and can never die again. When He died, He paid the penalty required to bring salvation to all who will believe and the penalty will never need to be paid again.

That means that if we ever lost our salvation, in order to be saved again, Jesus would have to die again.

Sometimes we will receive coupons in the mail for certain products, and many times those coupons will say something like "Good for one product only." In the same way, when Jesus died and paid the penalty for sin, having put our faith in what Jesus did for us is like the Bible says, "Good for one salvation only." That means that if our salvation doesn't last, then we would have to get another sacrifice, which is the very reason you will never find anyone in the Bible who got saved twice. We can't be saved twice because "by a single offering He has perfected for all time those who are being sanctified."

Furthermore, we are secure in Christ because the Lord always finishes what He begins. Look with me at Philippians 1:6, "And I am sure of this, that he who began a good work in you will bring it to completion at the day of Jesus Christ." Notice the phrase "he who began a good work." That's the Holy Spirit. What He began He will complete.

Let me tell you what the Holy Spirit did for your salvation. First, He convicted you of your sin. John 16:8 says, "And when he comes, he will convict the world concerning sin and righteousness and judgment." He did that for you. Second, the Holy Spirit is the converter. He worked to perform a miracle in your heart. The convictor and the converter is also the completer. "He who began a good work in you will bring it to completion." There is no possible way that God will never finish what He started because if He doesn't finish, that means He fails, and God can't fail anything. I don't know about you, but I have started a number of things in my life that I haven't completed, and in that sense, I have failed. Some of those things I started I will never complete. However, God doesn't fail what He begins, and He will complete the salvation that He began in us.

The fourth reason we are secure is that we are in Christ. Look at 2 Corinthians 5:17, "Therefore, if anyone is in Christ, he is a new creation. The old has passed away; behold, the new has come." When we accept the Lord as our Savior, the Bible says that we are in Christ. That means that we are part of the body of Christ. It also means that if a true believer were to be lost, a part of the body would be lost.

Our relationship as believers with God is a bit like Noah in the ark. If Noah went down during the flood, it would have been because the ark went down because Noah was in the ark. The Bible indicates that the ark is a picture of Christ, and when Noah went into the ark, God shut the door. When He shut the door, not only did He shut the water out, but also, He shut Noah and his family in. Now when Noah was in the ark, he may have fallen down many times while he was in there and while the waves of the flood were pushing the ark here and there, but he never fell out of the ark. Why? Because he was in Christ and God shut the door.

The Bible says in Ephesians 1:13, "In him you also, when you heard the word of truth, the gospel of your salvation, and believed in him, were sealed with the promised Holy Spirit." You see, Noah wasn't outside the ark hanging onto a peg, but he was inside the ark depending on God. I fear that some people think they are secure in Christ because they have written their names on the membership role of a church, or that they are secure because they follow a certain religion, or that they are secure because their parents were in the church choir. However, our security is not based on an institution or a belief system or on someone else's service but on a person, and His name is Jesus. If you are in Jesus, you are secure. If you are not in Jesus, you are not secure. It is as simple as that.

Fifth, we are secure because we already have eternal life. Let's go to John 5:24, "Truly, truly, I say to you, whoever hears my word and believes him who sent me has eternal life. He does not come into judgment, but has passed from death to life." Let me ask you a question. Have you believed in and put your full trust in Jesus alone for your salvation? Have you heard His Word and have you entrusted your life to God, your king and master? If you have, then the Bible says you have everlasting life right now. Everlasting life is not something you get when you die, but it is something you get when you receive Jesus as your Lord.

Look at John 5:24 again. In order to understand the words of Jesus, we need to get the tenses correct. We are not going to pass from death into life, but Jesus said that we *have* passed from death into life. If you have entrusted your life into the loving hands of the

Savior, you will never die. Jesus said in John 11:26, "And everyone who lives and believes in me shall never die." If we are in Christ, our bodies may cease to function for a while, but we cannot die because we have everlasting life.

In our home kitchen we have a set of knives made by a very reputable knife company. There was a day when I was a salesman for this knife company, and I sold enough knives to customers to win an entire set of kitchen knives. We wouldn't have ever been able to afford them had I not won them. One of the advantages of this particular brand of knives is that they carry a lifetime guarantee. That means that if a blade breaks, the company will replace the knife. If they do not keep a sharp edge, you can send them to the company, and they will sharpen them for you free of charge. However, if after ten years you lose a knife, that brings an end of the lifetime guarantee. If you lose it, the guarantee ends.

With Jesus, He gives an eternal guarantee. If you lose your life in any way, the guarantee never ends. It is a forever guarantee. Jesus said, "Whoever hears my word and believes him who sent me has eternal life."

Another reason we are secure in Christ is that Jesus is forever interceding for us. We find this promise in John 17:9, "I am praying for them. I am not praying for the world but for those whom you have given me, for they are yours." It is clear that Jesus is praying for the ones the Father has given to Him. What is He praying for them? We find the answer in verse 15, "I do not ask that you take them out of the world, but that you keep them from the evil one." The Lord prayed that prayer over 2,000 years ago, and He offered that prayer for His apostles Peter, James, and John, and the others. But He didn't pray that for you and me. He just prayed that prayer for them.

Wait, however. Let me show you something that will make you say hallelujah. In verse 20, we read, "I do not ask for these only, but also for those who will believe in me through their word." If you are looking at your Bible and you see that verse, if you don't mind writing in your Bible, you should write your name beside that verse. Right there we are told that Jesus is praying for you and for me. He prayed, "Father, not only do I pray for my disciples, but I pray for those who will believe down in [name the town where you live], and for those who attend [name the church body you belong to]. I pray for them also." He prayed that prayer because He knows the truth of 1 Peter 5:8, "Be sober-minded; be watchful. Your adversary the devil prowls around like a roaring lion, seeking someone to devour." You see, Satan's primary task in this world is to kill, steal, and destroy. If he can gain a stronghold in the church, then he can dramatically affect the kingdom of God. That's why the apostle Paul exhorts us in Ephesians 4:27, "And give no opportunity to the devil." To give opportunity means to allow him to gain a foothold in our lives. When you give the devil a foothold into your life, he takes a stronghold. That means that if you give Satan control of even one little part of your life, he'll soon take over the whole thing. If you give him a foothold into your life, he will turn it into a stronghold. That means we need to be careful about our thought life, our habits, and the indulgences of the world we might give in to.

During WWII, on D-Day, allied forces landed on the beaches of Normandy. It was critical that they establish a foothold on the beach that would allow them to set up a staging area to bring in more men and equipment for the battle. From that tiny foothold, the allied forces were able to push inland in an effort to liberate France. Except that Satan does not want to liberate you. He wants to establish a beachhead in your life so that he can take more and more of you. Once he gets deep enough into an area of sin, he turns the foothold into a stronghold, and that makes it harder for you to take back control of your life.

How does Satan get a foothold? Well, Ephesians 4 talks about how anger can be a foothold if you don't deal with it. It could also take the form of resentment, worry, lust, drugs, or even workaholism. If any of these things gain a foothold and establish a beachhead in your life, it can devastate you by taking control of you. That's why Jesus prayed for us. He asked that we might be kept. And as long as we yield to Him and flee from the devil, He will keep us from the devil's devouring ways.

However, you ask, what if I give the devil a foothold? What then? Will I lose my salvation? Based on everything you have read in this chapter, what do you think my answer will be? Remember Romans 8:39? Nothing is able to separate us from the love of God. Just because our son committed a terrible act by taking his life did he cease being my son? Absolutely not. He will always be our son, and we will always love him. In the same way, if you are truly a son or daughter of God, through faith in Jesus Christ, nothing can separate you from His love.

Now there are some people who say this is a dangerous doctrine because if people believe that once saved always saved, then they won't walk close to the Lord. But let me illustrate it this way. What if a child believed that if they disobeyed their parents they would be kicked out of the family? So one day he's good and he's in the family, and the next day his behavior is bad and he's out. He's in, then out, in, then out. What kind of a neurotic child would that be? No, what that child needs to learn is that if he disobeys his parents he is going to be disciplined. He needs to know, however, that he will always be a part of that family because Mom and Dad loves him. We don't serve God out of fear but out of love.

Somebody else might think that they can get saved and then sin all they want because God will never kick them out. But let me tell you that I am a man who sins more than I want to, and if you have a religion that says you can sin all you want to, then you don't know the Bible and you don't know my God. The truth is that when we get saved, we get our "want-er" fixed. As a matter of fact we get a brand-new "want-er." Our natural sinful nature and the devil will tempt us to sin, and sometimes we will yield to it, but we do what we don't want to do.

*****

*Barbara*

July 1, 2017 caught us off guard like nothing else in our lives to that point. The amazing gift is that Nathan's death did not catch God off guard. Just a few weeks before that horrible day, John 10:10 came to mind in my quiet time with the Lord. "The thief comes only to steal and kill and destroy. I came that they may have life and have it abundantly." Thinking back now, I find it amazing that it would seem that God was preparing me for something I had no idea was heading my way. As early as the evening of July 1 and over the course of the next few days, I remember saying to more than one person, "The thief came and he stole from us, he even killed one of our own, but he did not destroy." I knew in my heart, not just the protective and loving heart of a mother, but in the depths of me that Nathan was with the Lord. He literally passed from this life into the presence of His Savior. And in his darkest moment, even then, nothing was separating him from the love of God.

Did I ever have doubts? I mean, this was suicide, not an accident. No, I didn't. I have a very good memory. Sometimes I wish it wasn't so good. But because of my memory, I was able to go back through the totality of Nathan's life and see the consistency of how he chose to live and how his growth in his Christian life was ongoing. More importantly, God's Word had been consistently a part of my own life, and it was the knowledge of God's truth, accompanied by the Spirit, working in my own life that in the midst of such deep pain, I was able to draw comfort as I knew where Nathan was and comfort from my God to walk the ugly path of grief.

It's wonderful to be saved by grace. But it's even more wonderful to be saved and to know that we are saved. It's even more wonderful to be saved, to know we are saved, and to know that we can never lose our salvation.

If you are saved, then rejoice in your salvation. If you aren't saved, I encourage you to place your trust and hope in Jesus Christ, even if you feel like you wouldn't be able to live it. Because when you cast yourself on Jesus, He will never leave you or forsake you and He will carry you through. It won't be because you are holding on to Him, but because He is holding on to you.

Was our son Nathan saved unto eternal life, even after taking his own life? Yes, he is because he genuinely trusted in Christ as his Savior and demonstrated the fruit of the Spirit in His life. His faith has saved him for an eternity.

# I Know That I Know

## 1 John 5:5–13

How do you know something or anything at all? How do you know that it is time to eat something? You know because your body gives evidence of it. You know because your stomach starts to rumble and feel empty. You know because you start to feel weak in the knees. How do you know that it is nighttime and not day? You know because the sun gives evidence of it. We know instinctively that if it is dark outside, it is probably nighttime. How do you know that you love a person to the point that you want to marry them? I know, that's the age-old question, right? You know because when you are around them, you get sweaty palms. You know because you can't stop thinking about them during the day. You know because when you are with them, you are comfortable and you feel loved and you can't imagine not living for the rest of your life without them.

You see, we know things because there is evidence that give us the ability to know, and without the evidence you can't really say that you know for sure. In fact, what do we call it when we say we believe something is true, but we don't have the evidence to back it up? Evolution! Oh, sorry, I mean theory. Okay, evolution! People have theories about all kinds of things that they don't have empirical evidence to back up. Some people believe there may be life out there somewhere on other planets, so they theorize about what that life might be like, but there is no real evidence. I suppose that is why space agencies spend billions of dollars on space exploration. They are attempting to prove a theory by gathering evidence. Some people make theories about various scientific experiments, but until they can back it up with evidence, it will always be theory.

What about salvation? Is it just a theory that someone can be saved and know they are saved, or is there any evidence that can back it up? I have talked with hundreds of people about salvation, and the most common answer I get from people is "You can't know for sure." Based on what fact? Can you prove that you can never know?

For those of us who are experiencing the pain of a loved one who has passed from this life, this is a very relevant question. As a pastor of nearly forty years, I have performed dozens of funerals for people. I can safely say that in every one of those funerals, regardless of how the deceased person had lived their life or no matter what their belief system was, the hope, and sometimes the confidence, within the loved ones left behind was that the deceased had entered heaven into the presence of God and that they would see them again someday. I have always asked myself, upon what evidence do they have such hope?

In this chapter I want to show you from Scripture the facts that will demonstrate that we can know that we know that we are saved from sin and will someday enter into the presence of God.

The reason this subject is so important is because if you are saved, you ought to know it. If you are not saved, you need to be saved so that you can know it. The truth is that you can know beyond a shadow of a doubt that you are saved, and I am going to show you the empirical evidence as found in 1 John 5:5–13. Verse 5 begins, "Who is it that overcomes the world except the one who believes that Jesus is the Son of God?" John's Gospel (as in Matthew, Mark, Luke, John) was written to tell us how to get saved. However, John's first epistle tells us how to know we are saved. If you are ever so inclined, if you take a pen and circle all the words *know* that are found in 1 John, you will discover there are over forty of them. You see, this is good news of certainty. It is not a hope-so, but a know-so salvation. John wants us to be able to say "Hallelujah, I know that I'm heaven-bound."

Another key word in verses 5 to 13 is the word *witness*. In other translations you might see this word as *record, testimony*, or *testify*. You will find it recorded ten times. You see, John is giving us a witness, a record, a testimony for how we can know we are saved. The source of our certainty is a threefold cord not easily broken.

The first cord is the atoning work of the Savior. In speaking of the crucifixion of Jesus, John records in the Gospel of John 19:33–34, "But when they came to Jesus and saw that he was already dead, they did not break his legs. But one of the soldiers pierced his side with a spear, and at once there came out blood and water." Contrast what John went on to say later in his epistle in 1 John 5:6, "This is he who came by water and blood—Jesus Christ; not by the water only but by the water and the blood. And the Spirit is the one who testifies because the Spirit is the truth." When the soldier pierced the side of Jesus with the spear in an effort to puncture the heart, blood and water came out. John records this incident in both his gospel and his epistle. This must have been very important for John to have recorded it twice. The reason it is so important is because blood cleanses from sin. Hebrews 9:22 says that "without the shedding of blood there is no forgiveness of sins." The word *forgiveness* or *remission* in other translations means to discharge or to set free.

Why did someone have to die in order to pay the penalty of sin? That seems to be an extreme measure. The answer is because of the majesty of an infinite God. Habakkuk 1:13a says, "You who are of purer eyes than to see evil and cannot look at wrong," Revelation 4:8b, in describing God, says, "Holy, holy, holy, is the Lord God Almighty, who was and is and is to come!" And Psalm 97:2b says, "Righteousness and justice are the foundation of his throne." You see, every sin defies the majesty of an infinite God so that no matter how measureless His love is for us, our sin has to be taken away, for we could never stand before an infinite God in our sin. What we tend to forget is that when Jesus shed His blood on the cross, He ended the need to shed any more blood. At that point, the entire Old Testament sacrificial system ended. Furthermore, when Christ rose from the dead He rose to a newness of life, which we also will experience when we go to be with Him forever. The death of Christ brought about the removal of the penalty for sin for all those who will put their faith in what Jesus did on the cross.

Furthermore, water continues to cleanse. The water speaks of sanctification or, to say it another way, the cleansing from the pollution of sin. Jesus saves us from the wrath of God through His blood, and then He makes us pure by the water.

Apart from the blood and the water, we have no hope of heaven. As the old hymn so clearly states:

> Rock of Ages, cleft for me,
> Let me hide myself in Thee;
> Let the water and the blood,
> From Thy wounded side which flowed,
> Be of sin the double cure,
> Save from wrath and make me pure.
> Not the labor of my hands
> Can fulfill Thy law's demands;
> Could my zeal no respite know,
> Could my tears forever flow,
> All for sin could not atone;
> Thou must save, and Thou alone.
> Nothing in my hand I bring,
> Simply to Thy cross I cling;
> Naked, come to Thee for dress;
> Helpless, look to Thee for grace;
> Foul, I to the fountain fly;
> Wash me, Savior, or I die.
> While I draw this fleeting breath,
> When my eyes shall close in death,
> When I rise to worlds unknown,
> And behold Thee on Thy throne,
> Rock of Ages, cleft for me,
> Let me hide myself in Thee.

The third cord that gives us certainty for our salvation is the abiding witness of the Spirit. First John 5:6b describes it when John wrote, "And the Spirit is the one who testifies because the Spirit is the truth." He continues in verses 9 to 10a, "If we receive the testimony of men, the testimony of God is greater, for this is the testimony of God that he has borne concerning his Son. Whoever believes in the Son of God has the testimony in himself." Notice first that the Holy Spirit witnesses to you. That means that the Holy Spirit reveals to you whether your salvation is true or not. God wants us to be certain of our salvation without question, and He gives witness to the truth by the spirit of God.

Therefore, now we have three witnesses as to our salvation. We have the blood, the water, and the Spirit, and they are all in agreement with one another. The Old Testament law required the testimony of two or three witnesses to establish the truth of a particular matter. The word *witness* comes from a Greek word that refers to someone who has a personal and immediate knowledge of something. Even before we were saved, the Holy Spirit was telling us about Jesus. John 16:13a says, "When the Spirit of truth comes, he will guide you into all the truth." And John 15:26 declares, "But when the Helper comes, whom I will send to you from the Father, the Spirit of truth, who proceeds from the Father, he will bear witness about me." That means that everything Jesus did here on earth, the spirit of God testifies is true, and He testified to this truth through the spoken words of the apostles and those who followed Jesus by giving them the very words to say. He also testifies to the truth by making it possible for us to hear the truth. In other words, He orchestrates people and events in such a way that we are able to hear about salvation through Jesus Christ.

Furthermore, the Spirit witnesses to you, but He also witnesses in you. First John 5:10a says, "Whoever believes in the Son of God has the testimony in himself." When we accept Christ as Savior, the Holy Spirit takes up residence inside of us and now we have a witness within.

You never really know someone unless you are able to stay in their home with them. We can know each other casually. We can go out for coffee with one another and talk about the kids and the weather and what is happening in sports. However, we don't really know one another deeply because we don't live with one another. Every married couple understands exactly what I am talking about. When you were engaged, you were thinking about what married life would be like and you had all kinds of ideals about how happy you would be together and everything would be perfect. Then you got married. Very quickly you found out that your husband was kind of a slob and left stuff lying everywhere. In addition, you found out that she spends a lot more time in the bathroom than you expected. And she cries a lot. And she doesn't cook that well. And she doesn't like your feet on the coffee table. And he watches too many sports programs. And he's not as romantic as he was when you were dating.

Here is the point. Although God knows everything, and although He really does know all about us, we don't know Him until He comes to live with us. The Bible says that the Spirit gives witness to our spirit that we are children of God. I'm not talking about an emotional feeling, but I'm talking about a certainty. If you live by your emotions, you will be on a roller coaster and your assurance will go up and down with your emotions. However, the witness of the Spirit is deeper than emotions. Emotions are fine, but they are not the witness of the Spirit.

How does the Spirit give us this witness if not by emotions? Read Romans 8:15–16, "For you did not receive the spirit of slavery to fall back into fear, but you have received the Spirit of adoption as sons, by whom we cry, 'Abba! Father!' The Spirit himself bears witness with our spirit that we are children of God." The Spirit's witness is our inner confidence that we belong to Christ. It is not a confidence we work up in ourselves, but it is a confidence God gives to us.

Finally, He witnesses to us through the Word, the Bible. As we read His Word, He speaks to us and teaches us. That leads us to the third cord of confidence of our salvation.

The third cord is the Word of the Father. By now I hope you can see the threefold cord of your assurance of salvation, which is the Father, Son, and Holy Spirit together bringing you certainty.

First John 5:11–12 continues, "And this is the testimony, that God gave us eternal life, and this life is in his Son. Whoever has the Son has life; whoever does not have the Son of God does not have life." God gave us a record to read, which is the Bible. Where do we learn about the water and the blood and the witness of the Spirit but from the Word of God? It is essential that we believe the Word of God because it is the one central message in two words, from Genesis to Revelation, which is that *Jesus saves!* The Bible wasn't written to tell us how the heavens go, but it was written to tell us how to go to heaven. God gave us the Word so that we can have absolute assurance of our eternal life, and the divine, inspired Word of God is settled in heaven. Psalm 119:89 tells us, "Forever, O Lord, your word is firmly fixed in the heavens."

It is the atoning work of Christ, the abiding witness of the Spirit, and the affirming Word of God put together that enables us to say, "I know that I have eternal life."

Suppose you and your wife filed a joint income tax return. Let's say that the revenue office comes back and says, "You haven't proven you are married. We want some proof." So you write back with the message that says, "Oh, I remember the emotion I had and the joy and the commitment." In response, the revenue office says, "For our records, that won't count. Do you have something better?" So you dig out your marriage certificate, signed and attested to with a seal, and you send it to the revenue office with the note "Here is the record, sealed and attested to."

God has given us such a record as to our assurance of our salvation, which is His Word, and it goes beyond emotion.

The story is told of a little boy who was at a revival meeting and the pastor preached from John 5:24, "Truly, truly, I say to you, whoever hears my word and believes him who sent me has eternal life. He does not come into judgment, but has passed from death to life." The boy believed it and was saved. Yet all the way home he felt the devil whispering into his ear, "You're not saved. You don't feel just right. You don't deserve it. You're not good enough." All the way home, the devil was dogging his footsteps. He wasn't absolutely assured of his salvation, but he remembered the verse from the Bible the pastor was preaching from. So he looked it up in his Bible, and it said, "Truly, truly, I say to you." That means that it is true and that Jesus said it. He read on, "whoever hears my word." And the boy said to himself, "I heard it." The verse continues, "and believes him who sent me." He said, "I believe." Finally, the verse says, "has eternal life." To that, the boy said, "I have everlasting life. The Bible says so." However, that night it seemed like the devil was under his bed. So he took his Bible and opened it up to that verse from John and put it under his bed and said, "Devil, read it for yourself." And from that point on, his doubt left him.

I don't know if that story it true or not, but the truth of the story is on the mark. The principle is that when the devil gets on your trail, don't argue with him. Simply show him the Word of God and step out of the argument. Let him argue with God if he wants to.

Now I have heard people say to me, "Pastor, only God knows for sure who is saved and who is not saved." That is exactly right. The Bible says in 1 John 5:9, "If we receive the testimony of men, the testimony of God is greater, for this is the testimony of God that he has borne concerning his Son." The testimony of God is greater than what I am writing to you. It is what God is telling you. I cannot tell you whether you are saved or not, but you can be assured of your own salvation through the witness of the Father, the Son, and the Holy Spirit within you. You can be assured of your own salvation, and this will become evident for all of us to see.

CHAPTER

# When It Seems Like God Doesn't Answer Prayer

## 2 Corinthians 12:7–9

Have you ever been in a restaurant or in a public place and you see a group of people sitting with each other but they aren't talking to one another? Instead, they are looking at their smartphone. There is no communication happening between them, unless, I suppose, they send each other a text. Or worst yet, have you ever been in a conversation with someone and in the middle of the conversation they look at their phone, or their eyes drift somewhere else, or they make a totally unrelated comment that shows you they really weren't listening?

Perhaps there have been times in your life that you have felt that God isn't listening. You have been praying for an unsaved relative for years, and it seems like they just get farther and farther from the Lord. Or perhaps you have prayed for a good job, but the phone never rings. You have prayed for a sick relative that they would be healed, but God doesn't answer the way you've asked.

Feeling like God didn't listen was my thought after Nathan took his life. We raised him under a godly influence, the best we could in our own fallen nature. We prayed that he would grow to be a godly man and to serve the Lord in whatever occupation he chose. We prayed that God would send him a godly wife and that God would protect him and use him for His glory. It seemed as though God was answering our prayers for him. As I've already shared, Nathan attended two years of Bible school. He was serving the Lord. God sent to him a godly young lady whom he was engaged to marry, and he was serving the Lord in his secular job, living for Christ before those he worked with. We couldn't help but question what happened to our prayers. How could such a horrible thing happen, when we had so diligently asked God to cover this young man and keep him safe and to use him? It felt that God had not listened.

It is in those times that we cry out with the psalmist in Psalm 10:1, "Why, O Lord, do you stand far away? Why do you hide yourself in times of trouble?" And for those who are in pain, a theoretical answer just won't do. It will not suffice just to say, "God always answers prayer. Sometimes He says yes. Sometimes He says no. Sometimes He says wait." We say that a lot, don't we? I have said it myself. However, it sounds so shallow when we are crying out to God from the depths of our heart and it feels like the heavens are brass and the answer never comes.

Also, there are people who bear hidden scars from the pain of unanswered prayer. They remember the times when they prayed, and they said all the right words with all the right motives. They even asked their friends to join them in prayer. Then they waited, and waited, and waited, but God never seemed to answer.

We don't talk about this problem very much. Maybe it is because we feel like if we talk about our own unanswered prayers, it might cause others to lose their own faith in God. Or maybe we don't talk about it because we feel like it might make us look like a spiritual weakling.

You wouldn't think this kind of subject would make a comic strip, but I happened upon a comic strip of Calvin and Hobbes. In the comic, it is late November and a little boy is waiting with his sled for the first big snowfall. He waits and waits, but all he finds is brown grass. So he says, "If I was in charge, we'd never see grass between October and May." And then looking to the heavens he says, "On three, ready? One...two...three...snow." Nothing happens, and he is downcast. Then the little boy shouts to the heavens, "I said snow! C'mon! Snow!" Thoroughly disgusted with God's failure, he says, "Okay then, don't snow! See what I care! I like the weather! Let's have it forever." However, his defiance doesn't last, and in the next frame we see him on his knees praying, "Please snow, please? Just a foot. Okay, eight inches, that's all. Come on, even six inches." And he looks to heaven and says, "I'm waiting." Finally, we see him running around with clenched fists making noises until he is totally exhausted with no snow in sight. He looks up to God and cries out, "Do you want me to become an atheist?"

That's a great picture of a lot of Christians today, except that they have prayed for more important things than snow, but the end result has been the same. In frustration and despair, they cry out to God, "Do you want me to become an atheist?" And some have, but most haven't. However, they keep the pain locked up inside, still believing in a God who sometimes answers prayer and sometimes doesn't, at least not in the way they want Him to answer.

If this is a description of you, it might be helpful for you to know that you are not the only one who has had prayer go unanswered in the way you prayed. I'm one of those recipients of seemingly unanswered prayers, and the Bible is filled with stories of men and women who prayed to God in times of crises, yet for reasons that were explained sometimes and were not explained at other times, God didn't answer their prayers. We don't hear about that very much because we like hearing about when great answers come in the nick of time.

Most of us would rather hear about the Red Sea parting than about Trophimus being left sick by Paul in Miletus. We would rather hear about the walls of Jericho tumbling down by the hand of God than about Stephen being stoned to death. Those miracles that did happen are a lot more encouraging than miracles that almost happened.

However, as I turn through the pages of my Bible, I don't find any story more encouraging to me than the account of the apostle Paul's unanswered prayer found in 2 Corinthians 12. In the same passage, Paul tells us about how fourteen years earlier, he was caught up into heaven and had seen things that no mortal man had ever seen. It was the greatest experience of his life, and he never forgot what it was like. However, when that great experience was over, he experienced something else that would change his whole perspective in life. Look at the story beginning in verse 7, "So to keep me from becoming conceited because of the surpassing greatness of the revelations, a thorn was given me in the flesh, a messenger of Satan to harass me, to keep me from becoming conceited."

We are never told what Paul's thorn in the flesh was. I suspect if we knew we would most likely overidentify with the thorn and miss the lesson. What I want us to see is that Paul prayed for God to remove the thorn so that he could get on with his ministry and get on with his life. Perhaps you have felt the same way at times. "If I could just get rid of this [fill in the blank], life would be so much better and I could serve God so much better." The problem is that some of us have been given a thorn that is impossible to get rid of. It's the thorn of loss. It's a thorn that will never work its way loose until the resurrection. What do we do about that kind of thorn? Paul prayed three times for his thorn to be removed, which tells me that his affliction was something that could have been remedied by God. It was something God could have healed, or removed, or changed in his life. Yet every time Paul prayed about it, God answered with a no.

It's not exactly correct to say that God didn't answer Paul's prayer. And by the way, I believe God always answers our prayers. But in Paul's case, the answer was something other than what he requested. God told him in verse 9, "My grace is sufficient for you." Paul was perhaps the greatest Christian who ever lived. He was the person who introduced Christianity to Europe. He wrote thirteen of the twenty-seven books of the New Testament. Yet when this great man prayed about a need in his life, he discovered that God did not and would not answer his prayers. It is even hard to comprehend since we know that Paul was a man of prayer. He wrote about prayer in all his letters. He encouraged all his churches to pray.

Imagine if Paul showed up at one of our church services and he offered to pray for us individually, no matter how long it took. What would you do? I don't know about you, but I would be the first one in line. I might even knock you over to get the best place in line. Yet here is a clear-cut case, given in his own words, of a time in Paul's own life when he desperately begged God repeatedly to answer a very specific prayer yet God gave him an emphatic no.

As I read his story, I find several important lessons we can learn. One lesson is that unanswered prayers happen to even mature Christians. This isn't something that happens just to the undeserving. It doesn't happen just to sinners. But it happens to people you would think should be the very ones who deserve to get an answer. It happens to people who are serving the Lord, who are dedicated to living for Him, and who are growing in their relationship with Christ. Don't allow this to be a discouragement to you. Keep reading, and you will come to the good part.

Another lesson is when unanswered prayers happen, it is humanly unexplainable. God didn't give Paul a reason for His no answer except that he would have to be content with God's grace. Many times when God says no we feel like He is being unfair or maybe He didn't understand what we were asking or how difficult our situation is. We feel abandoned and alone. We may even feel like God didn't hear our prayer at all. This leads us to the third lesson.

*****

*Barbara*

Just over three and a half years on our grief journey, probably the most important lesson that has become clearer each day is that to be encouraged by God's presence and His Word, I have to spend time with God and I have to know the Word. And to know the Word, I have to be in it—literally as often as I have sensed the need. Three and a half years later, I still don't understand perfectly why God allowed Nathan to complete suicide. But God's Word has permeated my very being, mind, and soul. Verses that I learned when I was school age have often reverberated through my mind, when I come to that place of saying again and again, "I just don't get it." Two simple little verses in Proverbs, chapter 3, 5, and 6, "Trust in the Lord with all your heart and lean not on your own understanding. In all your ways, acknowledge Him and He will direct your paths." *Lean not on your own understanding* has been on repeat through this time. It may sound simple. In fact the truth is the hard part is living it. Yes, God gives me grace every single day, but He also gives me a choice and how I decide. He leaves me to decide how I will choose. The amazing thing is that over time of preaching God's truth to myself, I have come to a peace. I still don't get it, and that is okay. The reality is that I am of an era in history where we have an abundance of information at our fingertips and an expectation that we should know all and understand all, yet I am still human and will never understand all that goes on in this world.

*****

When God doesn't answer our prayers, it is because He has a higher purpose in mind. In Paul's case, he kept on praying until God gave him an explanation in verse 9, "But he said to me, 'My grace is sufficient for you, for my power is made perfect in weakness.' Therefore I will boast all the more gladly of my weaknesses." You see, sometimes our prayers are not answered because God can do more through us by not answering than by answering. Sometimes God's *no* is better than His *yes*. Think of it this way. Suppose God answered all your prayers all the time, exactly the way you prayed? For just a minute, let's forget the fact that some of our prayers are foolish and short-sighted, but let's just suppose that God answered all of them. Would that produce any kind of spiritual maturity in our lives? You might say, "No, but it sure would be awesome!" No, not so awesome because eventually our trust would be in the answer and not the Lord. However, when God says no, we are forced to decide whether we will still trust in God alone with the benefit of an answered prayer to lean on. Now don't get me wrong. No matter how God answers our prayer, it's wonderful. We all want a yes from God, and if none of our prayers were answered with a yes, we would probably stop praying. However, if all our prayers were answered exactly the way we prayed them, we would end up taking God for granted. Therefore, prayer always forces us to trust in God alone, and when we do that, God alone gets the glory because it is at that point that His strength is made perfect in weakness. To say it another way, we grow best in the darkness.

Do I wish that our son was still alive today? Absolutely! I would give anything for that to have happened. I would have spared nothing to help Nathan with whatever he was going through to keep him alive. My prayer for Nathan to prosper and be safe and grow spiritually feels like an unanswered prayer, and I struggled in my heart with that for many months. Why would God say no to my prayer? It is not because He is an unloving, evil God who relishes in my misery. Instead, His purpose is to develop my trust in Him no matter what valleys of dark shadows I go through. His grace must be sufficient; otherwise my dependence would be on my answered prayers instead of on God Himself.

Author and commentator William F. Buckley once made the comment in an interview, "As an old man, looking back on one's life, it's one of the things that strike you most forcibly—that the only thing that's taught one anything is suffering. Not success, not happiness, not anything like that. The only thing that really teaches one what life is about—the joy of understanding, the joy of coming in contact with what life really signifies—is suffering, affliction." And that's exactly what Paul is talking about. He is saying that we grow best in the darkness of pain, sadness, and despair. Oh, we learn a lot of things in the sunlight, but we grow best in the darkness.

Furthermore, we learn from Paul that when we pray, we tend to focus exclusively on the answers. However, God wants us to focus on Him. Whatever will help us focus on God is what we need. That means that our prayers will be answered in ways we would have never expected and sometimes didn't ask for or even want. At other times God may simply delay in giving an answer. Do you remember the experience of Job? He lost his home, his fortune, his children, his health, and his reputation. Everything he counted as dear to him was taken away. He finally hit rock bottom and was filled with anger and wished that he was dead or that he had never been born in the first place. Then he said these words, found in Job 13:15a, "Though he slay me, I will hope in him." In other words, "You can take my life, but you can't make me stop trusting You." You can sense a bit of belligerent defiance in his words. No, he was not happy at all about what God had allowed to be done to him, and he still wanted his day in court, yet underneath the anger and the pain was a bedrock of faith in God. That's the place where God wants to bring us, and frankly, sometimes the only way He can get us there is through prayer answered with a no or wait. Yet having said all that, we still need to know how to respond when our prayers are not answered as we expected.

*****

## Barbara

Another well-known family in Scripture is Mary, Martha, and Lazarus. I have often thought of them as well over these last few years in that they were well-known and loved by Jesus, but even as Jesus heard that Lazarus was very ill, he did not rush to visit and heal him. He took his time. What were his words to his disciples? "This sickness will not end in death. No, it is for God's glory so that God's Son may be glorified through it" (John 11:4). And then just prior to him raising Lazarus from the dead, he said in verse 40, "Did I not tell you that if you believed, you would see the glory of God?" Hmmm. As much as I don't understand why Nathan was permitted to leave us, I do know that God does not waste anything in our lives. As Jesus lived and walked this earth, His desire was always to draw people to His Father and for God to be glorified. As Mark has said, we so wish that our lives had not had to take this path of grief, but I do know that I have grown to know and see and love my heavenly father in a way that I never knew before. And oh, how I wish and pray that others would know Him in their hearts in a fresh and deep way— ways that the world can never ever fill for them. The reality is that I do not know how Nathan's suicide can bring glory to our God. But I do know that I do not need to understand. I do accept the truth of Isaiah 55:8–9, which says, "'For my thoughts are not your thoughts, neither are your ways my ways,' declares the LORD. 'As the heavens are higher than the earth, so are my ways higher than your ways and my thoughts than your thoughts.'"

*****

Let me offer three responses to unexpected answers to prayer. First, keep on praying. Jesus said in Luke 18:1, "And he told them a parable to the effect that they ought always to pray and not lose heart." Note the phrase "to pray and not lose heart." Sometimes God's answers are delayed for reasons beyond our comprehension. We do not know why God says no 999 times and then says yes to the thousandth prayer. Don't be ashamed to keep going back to the throne room of God with the same request. We keep on praying because we don't know when God might say yes.

Second, give God the right to say no. I know that ultimately God already has that right, whether we acknowledge it or not. But if we never acknowledge that God has the right to say no to us, then we will probably be filled with anger and frustration. Jesus Himself gave us an example of this in the garden, just before His arrest. He prayed in Matthew 26:39, "And going a little farther he fell on his face and prayed, saying, 'My Father, if it be possible, let this cup pass from me; nevertheless, not as I will, but as you will.'" He was saying, "Father, if there is another way, I will take it. But I'll do whatever you want." Now if Jesus needed to pray that way, how much more do we? Let's let God be God and let's give Him the right to say no.

Third, keep on doing what you know to be right. The apostle Paul wrote to the Philippian Church from prison, and he says in Philippians 1:21, "For to me to live is Christ, and to die is gain." In other words, he was saying, "I know that I am in this prison cell for doing the right thing, and I don't know when I will be getting out, but I am going to keep doing the right thing as long as I live. After the missionary Jim Elliot was murdered in the jungle, his widow, Elizabeth, began living by the mantra "Do the next thing." It comes from an old Saxon poem. In her autobiography she talks about applying this in her missionary work. Even though covered in grief, what is the next thing for you to do?

When you feel like God isn't answering prayer, keep on praying, keep on believing, keep on reading the Bible, keep following the Lord because if you follow the Lord in the darkness, eventually the light will shine again and you will be glad you didn't give up.

In 1932, A. M. Overton was a pastor of a church in Mississippi with a wife and three small children. His wife was pregnant with their fourth child, but when it came time for delivery, there were complications and both she and the baby died.

During the funeral service, the preacher officiating the service noticed that Pastor Overton was writing something on a piece of paper. He thought that was kind of odd, and after the service the minister asked him about it, and he handed him the paper with a poem he had just written, which he titled "He Maketh No Mistake." It is a poem that became known around the world, and it reads:

### He Maketh No Mistake

My Father's way may twist and turn
My heart may throb and ache,
But in my soul I'm glad to know,
He maketh no mistake.

My cherished plans may go astray,
My hopes may fade away,
But still I'll trust my Lord to lead,
For He doth know the way.
Tho' night be dark and it may seem
That day will never break,

I'll pin my faith, my all, in Him,
He maketh no mistake.
There's so much now I cannot see,
My eyesight's far too dim,

But come what may,
I'll simply trust and leave it all to Him.
For by and by the mist will lift,
And plain it all He'll make,
Through all the way, tho' dark to me,
He made not one mistake.

I believe that in the end, that will be the testimony of every child of God. When we finally get to heaven, we will finally see that through all the twists and turns of life, *God made not one mistake.* And in that day we will see there was a reason why God never said "My answers are sufficient" but that "My grace is sufficient for you."

# Why Does God Allow Tragedy and Suffering?

Suffering and tragedy abound in our world today. You can't turn on the news without hearing of another murder, a rape victim, another celebrity who has been caught with you name it, another political figure who has worked outside the bounds of the law, genocide, and hate crimes. The list can go on and on. I haven't even mentioned the tragedies that have occurred as a result of weather-related incidents. In addition, what about the tragedies that never are reported or that we never hear about in our local news.

All the tragedy and heartache prompt us to ask why God allows so much hardship and suffering in our world. Perhaps you are asking the same question on a personal level. Many times I have asked why God allowed Nathan to take his own life. It doesn't make any sense to me. God could have prevented it, but He didn't. Yet this is not a new question. It dates back thousands of years. In fact, it was asked in the Old Testament by a man named Job and by the writers of the Psalms. It was an especially relevant question during the twentieth century when we experienced two World Wars, the Holocaust, genocides in the Soviet Union and China, devastating famines in Africa, the killing fields of Cambodia, the emergence of AIDS, the genocide in Rwanda, the ethnic cleansing in Kosovo, and now into the twenty-first century we are living through a worldwide pandemic of a virus called COVID-19.

Why do these horrific things happen if there is a loving and powerful God? Furthermore, why do bad things happen to good people? It is a question so many of us ask, especially when tragedy hits our own homes. Jesus was honest about pain and suffering when He said in John 16:33, "I have said these things to you, that in me you may have peace. In the world you will have tribulation." In the world you will have tribulation. He didn't say that troubles might happen but that they will happen. But why? Why does God allow these bad things to happen? If you ask me why God allowed a man to kill twenty-six people in a church building, I would have to tell you that I do not know. I don't know why God allowed our son to take his own life. I don't have God's mind on such matters, and I don't have His perspective on this world.

This is why we are in need of gaining God's perspective on life as found in His Word. I can tell you that 1 Corinthians 13:12 says, "For now we see in a mirror dimly, but then face to face. Now I know in part; then I shall know fully, even as I have been fully known." There is a day coming when we will be able to see things with clarity. However, for now, many things that happen in our world and in our life are like driving through the fog. We cannot see and we cannot understand God's infinite perspective.

Frankly, people like my wife and I who have gone through tragedy don't need a theological explanation as to why evil exists in the world or why bad things happen to good people. Any kind of intellectual response simply falls on deaf ears. When people go through a tragedy, and what I have discovered in my own journey, we need the very real and comforting presence of God in our lives. In addition, we need other people who will surround us with love. Many times people are afraid to reach out to comfort those who have gone through tragedy for fear they might do or say the wrong thing. But the reality is you don't have to do or say anything. Your presence can be enough. Life becomes even more difficult when, after a tragedy, there is only silence.

In our experience, we received a lot of love and care the first month after Nathan's death, and then after that, understandably, other people went back to their own lives and routines and life resumed as normal for them. But we were left with a hole in our heart that will never be healed from our grief, and the silence of other people is deafening. When people never mention Nathan's name, when they avoid asking "How are you?" for fear of getting an honest answer, or when people avoid you altogether just because they don't know what to say or do, it brings further hurt and isolation and prevents healing from taking place. You see, people can become the presence of God in other's lives. As a pastor, when I walk into a hospital room of a dying person, with the family all around mourning their eventual loss, often I don't have many words to say except a comforting word from the Bible and a prayer. And yet I know that I have become the presence of Jesus in that hospital room. I am not Jesus, but I represent Him in a living way and simply my presence can bring comfort to hurting people.

Having said all that, I still believe it is important to grapple with the question of why God allows suffering in our lives. Even though we cannot understand everything about it, I believe we can understand some things about it. So let me take you to some truths from the Bible that can help to satisfy our hearts and souls.

First, let me remind you that God is not the creator of evil and suffering. People will ask me, "Why didn't God just create a world where tragedy and suffering didn't exist?" The answer is that He did. We're told in Genesis 1:31a, "And God saw everything that he had made, and behold, it was very good." When God created the world, He created a perfect environment without sin or corruption. He set Adam and Eve in a beautiful garden in a perfect environment and said to them, "Tend the garden and take care of things." In the beginning, there were no weeds to pull. The sun wasn't too hot, and the nights were not too cold. It truly was a paradise. Furthermore, all the animals were still friendly and tame. In addition, Adam and Eve had a perfect, harmonious relationship with God and one another.

When God created mankind He did so for no other reason than to express His love. However, to give us the ability to love, God also had to give us a free will to be able to decide whether to love or not to love. Why? Because love always involves a choice. God didn't create us with a drawstring on our neck that when you pull it, the words "I love you" come out. No, real love always involves choice. Therefore, in order for us to experience love, God created us with a free will.

Unfortunately, Adam and Eve exercised their free will by rebelling against God, and mankind has been exercising their free will by rebelling ever since. Did God foresee this would happen? Of course He did. However, He could also foresee that many people would choose to follow Him. And even though it cost God the price of His Son's suffering to accomplish redemption for our sins, it was worth it because those who chose to follow Christ have the hope of spending eternity with Him.

As we ponder the mystery of pain and evil, let's never forget that God didn't create it. It is easy to use God as a scapegoat when bad things happen in our world or to us personally, but we're pointing a finger at the wrong person.

Also, I would like to remind you that even though suffering is not good, God can use it to accomplish good. A passage of Scripture that Barbara and I have been claiming for ourselves is Romans 8:28 where God promises, "And we know that for those who love God all things work together for good, for those who are called according to his purpose." It is important to note that this verse does not say that God causes evil and suffering but that He promises to cause good to come out of it. Also, notice that this verse does not say we will always see how God might cause the good to come out of a bad situation, or that we will even see it in our lifetime, but that God will do it.

Remember when we looked at 1 Corinthians 13, we discovered that right now we only see things in this life dimly, as in a fog, but then face-to-face? Maybe in this life we will miss seeing the good. Maybe our vision is so blurred that we miss the good God is bringing about. However, one day it will all be clear and we will see the good that God is producing.

Furthermore, God does not make this promise to everyone. This is a promise He makes to those who are committed to following Him. There are many times when it is tempting to think that

God can't bring anything good out of the tragedy that has happened, whatever it may be. It may feel like the damage done is too great and too extreme and that the depth of our suffering is too much. But I think the words of an anonymous author can help us in our thinking

"God took the very worst thing that has ever happened in the history of the universe—the death of God on the cross—and turned it into the very best thing that has happened in the history of the universe: the opening up of heaven to all who follow Him."

If God can take the very worst circumstance imaginable and turn it into the very best situation possible, then He can certainly take the negative circumstances that happen in our lives and create something good from them. Furthermore, could it be that what the good God wants to bring about isn't even something tangible, something we can see or put our hands on, but perhaps the good God wants to bring about is for us to be conformed more in the likeness of Jesus Christ? We all agree that suffering is never good, but somehow God uses it for good.

I am also encouraged when I am reminded that the day is coming when suffering will cease and God will judge evil. The question that is in the mind of many people is that if God has the power to do away with evil, then why doesn't He just do it? However, there is a flaw in that question. Just because God hasn't put an end to evil in the world yet doesn't mean that He won't do it.

For example, let's say that I wrote a novel, and you buy it but read only half of the book. You put the book down and write me a note that says, "There are too many loose ends with the plot. You didn't resolve all the issues with the characters." I would write back to you and say, "But you only read half the book."

You see, the story of the world isn't over yet, and there is a day coming when sickness and pain will be eradicated and when people will be held accountable for the evil they have committed. What is holding God up from applying His justice? The answer is found in 2 Peter 3:9, "The Lord is not slow to fulfill his promise as some count slowness, but is patient toward you, not wishing that any should perish, but that all should reach repentance." The context of that verse is that there were some people who were questioning the second coming of the Lord, and they were saying that nothing had changed since the beginning of the world and that nothing would ever change. Peter responds by saying that the Lord is delaying His coming out of love for humanity. He is giving more people the opportunity to turn to Him for salvation. Be assured, however, that one day Christ will return, and when He does, He will clean up the mess we have made because of sin once and for all.

Let's also be reminded that our suffering today will pale in comparison to the good things God has in store for us in the future. Paul said in Romans 8:18, "For I consider that the sufferings of this present time are not worth comparing with the glory that is to be revealed to us." Keep in mind that this is the same man who had suffered through beatings, shipwrecks, imprisonments, rejection, hunger, thirst, and homelessness. Paul suffered through more pain than most of us will ever be required to endure. I don't want to minimize any of our own pain because I have had my fair share of it.

There was a three-year period in our lives when Barb broke her elbows falling down some stairs while she was seven months pregnant. Let your imagination take over for a minute. Can you imagine a seven months pregnant woman trying to crawl out of a waterbed with two broken elbows? And then there came chicken pox. First, Barb contracted them. As an adult this is very painful. Then all three boys contracted them. During the same time frame, Barb had surgery for a deviated septum, and Nathan was having ear infections and was diagnosed with asthma that took months to diagnose. And then there were five years of very difficult ministry. And yet during those years God also did some really wonderful things in our lives. We had a brand-new Dodge Van given to us. We had some terrific friends who treated us as family and loved our children. We look back on those years with fondness. If you were to ask us to tell you about our lives, we would probably tell you about all the wonderful things that had happened to us. Oh, we would remember the bad things, but all the other days that were good would far outweigh the other bad days.

Maybe that's a good analogy of heaven. This is not to deny the reality of our pain today. I will forever suffer with the grief of

Nathan's death with some days having it weigh heavier on me than others. And there are people who are suffering with physical ailments of every sort. Loved ones have passed away from various diseases. People are going through all kinds of trauma, and I cannot deny that all of it is very painful and difficult. Yet in heaven, after 354, 485, 545, 1,000 days of pure bliss and an infinite more to come, if someone asks you in heaven, "So, how has your existence been?" you will instantly reply, "It has been more than incredible. Words can't even describe how wonderful it is."

We had twenty-six wonderful years with our son Nathan. He brought so much joy to our lives. We look back at his growing up years with gladness in our hearts because he was such a joy to us. He had such a sensitive spirit. He was so kind and generous. He seemed to know when we were having a bad day, and he would come and give us a hug, not saying anything. Yet the pain that has been generated by his death is deep and lasting. My heart is continually broken and feels like a hole has been created in my life. This is not to say we are not fulfilled and grateful for our other two sons, their wives, and our four grandsons. They continue to bring much joy to us. But there is one missing from among us. Every time we have family gatherings, we are reminded that one is missing. One can live a pretty healthy life with a limb missing, but you always feel the pain and crippling effects of that missing limb. You are grateful for your other limbs, but you will always miss the limb that is gone.

Having said that, I can still attest to the goodness of God in all of this pain. Barb and I have grown closer as a husband and wife as we have gone through pain together and as we have struggled to find answers together. We have sensed the nearness of God unlike ever before. We are learning new dependence upon the Lord, learning to trust Him and love Him even more, though not having all the answers we would like to have. And there are years to come when we will experience other joys in life with our other children and grandchildren. Then when we arrive in our heavenly home, we will be rejoined with our beautiful son to live for an eternity together. I am sure that in a hundred years if you asked me how my existence has been, I will probably respond, "More than incredible."

Finally, let's be reminded that we decide whether to turn bitter or to turn to God for peace and courage when tragedy happens. I have personally witnessed people who have become bitter and turned from God when some difficult things happened to them. I've seen others who have gone through suffering who have become more dependent on God. The bottom line is that we have to make a choice as to what our response is going to be. We can either run away from God or run to Him.

When Nathan died we chose to run to God. Immediately we saw Nathan's suicide as an attack from the enemy, and our only choice was to run to God for refuge. We clung to passages from God's Word, like the words of Joseph when he told his brothers, "As for you, you meant evil against me, but God meant it for good" (Genesis 50:20). "The thief comes only to steal and kill and destroy. I came that they may have life and have it abundantly" (John 10:10). "And we know that for those who love God all things work together for good, for those who are called according to his purpose" (Romans 8:28). These passages and more are ones we continue to hang on to as promises from God.

*****

## Barbara

We are about halfway through this book. What you have read has been God's truth and a bit of our experience. It may seem that we have a Scripture verse for just about everything. It may seem that our journey of grief, which has left us shell-shocked for months, was simply addressed with reading a specific scripture and moving on with our day and with our life. Shockingly simple, incredibly difficult. I mentioned it earlier, and yet I think it bears repeating: to draw on God's Word and to find any comfort through God's Word, we must know it and we must be reading it. However, it isn't easy. For me, coming to that recognition had a profound effect on how I grieved. Grief is exhausting. It is exhausting for a number of reasons. The very first night of knowing that Nathan was no longer breathing on this earth, I did not sleep even for a minute. I was paralyzed with the pain. Three and a half years later, I have made a great deal of progress, but it has taken all this time to come to a new acceptance that my sleep patterns will be disrupted at those significant times of year and take many weeks to normalize again.

Nathan's birthday is in the month of May, along with Mother's Day. June 2017 was a month of celebration as he moved to his first apartment and I attended two wedding showers. On June 30, we were in Niagara Falls, ready to begin the celebration of Canada's 150th birthday. It was the very next day, around supper time, that we received the worst phone call of any parents' life. That time period covers about six weeks, but even as we began year four of "life without Nathan," it seemed I was well into the fall before I was sleeping reasonably well. Why do I share this minutia? I share it to encourage those of you who are struggling to be patient with the process and to encourage those who walk alongside of one struggling to ease up on expectations of what life should look like for them. Choosing to do the right things to bring healing takes time, more time than I wish, which has become my new reality. I don't understand the why, but I still get to choose to live the life well that God has blessed me with as long as I have breath.

*****

What happens when we run to God? Earlier in this chapter, I quoted John 16:33, but only the first part of that verse. Here is what the entire verse says, "I have said these things to you, that in me you may have peace. In the world you will have tribulation. But take heart; I have overcome the world." Jesus is offering two things we need most when we are hurting. He offers us peace to deal with our present problems. I can truthfully say that through all the pain and grief Barbara and I have suffered, we have truly experienced His peace. It is a difficult thing to describe to anyone who has never entered into this kind of pain, but it is a peace that you realize that without it, you could never make it through. It isn't visible. It isn't tangible, like someone giving you a hug. But it is something that wells up in you and keeps you steady in the storm. And secondly, Jesus is offering courage to deal with our future. How can He offer these things? Because as verse 33 says, "I have overcome the world." Through His death and resurrection, Jesus has deprived the world of its ultimate power over us so that now suffering and death doesn't have to be the last word because only God has the last word. This is what Habakkuk 3:17–19 is communicating: "Though the fig tree should not blossom, nor fruit be on the vines, the produce of the olive fail and the fields yield no food, the flock be cut off from the fold and there be no herd in the stalls, yet I will rejoice in the Lord; I will take joy in the God of my salvation. God, the Lord, is my strength; he makes my feet like the deer's; he makes me tread on my high places." The prophet is saying that even though everything about him seemed to be doom and gloom, he could still rejoice in the Lord because He has the final word.

Jesus conquered the world for us when He made the sacrifice by dying on a cross and raising from the dead. Someone once said, "God's ultimate answer to suffering isn't an explanation; it's the incarnation." As a result, our suffering demands a personal response from God, and He came to give us just that. If you are broken, remember that Jesus was broken for us. If you feel despised, remember that Jesus was despised and rejected of men. If you are crying out and feeling like you cannot take it anymore, remember that Jesus was a man of sorrows and acquainted with grief. If someone has betrayed you, remember that Jesus was sold out by a friend. If someone has turned from you, remember that men hid their faces from Him and He was despised.

Jesus descended into all our hells for us, and no matter how deep your darkness, He is deeper still and every tear you shed becomes His tear. However, Jesus does more than simply sympathize with our troubles. Any close friend can do that. Jesus is closer than your closest friend. If you have received Him as your Savior and Lord, He lives inside of you. Therefore, your sufferings become His sufferings. Your sorrow becomes His sorrow.

Therefore, we conclude that when tragedy strikes, when suffering visits, when you are wrestling with pain, when you make the choice to run into the arms of the Savior, what you will discover is peace to deal with the present. You will discover courage to deal with your future. And you will experience an incredible promise of eternal life in heaven.

CHAPTER

# Exposing Satan's War Plan

## 1 Timothy 1:18

Everyone of us today are in a war, but very few people are even aware that it's happening. Every day we turn on the news and hear about wars going on around the world. We hear about the war against ISIS. We hear about the war in Syria that has caused a refugee crisis. We hear of the wars in Pakistan, Myanmar, and the Ukraine. However, when was the last time you turned on the news and heard a report about the spiritual war that has been going on for thousands of years, has caused mass casualties, and is threatening to destroy lives every day?

John 10:10 tells us, "The thief comes only to steal and kill and destroy." The thief Jesus is referring to is none other than Satan and all his demons. Satan's only purpose in this world is to steal God's joy from people, to destroy people's lives, and even to kill people before they can enter into a relationship with Jesus Christ, or to remove Christians from the earth so that they cannot effectively serve Christ. We believe our son Nathan was in a spiritual war that eventually took his life. Nathan was a genuine servant of the Lord and had so much potential for making an impact for the sake of Christ. He was serving in winter Christian camps and was planning to become a missionary in camping ministry. He served in the youth ministry of our church, and he was constantly helping his friends with whatever needs they had, whether that be helping someone to move or helping someone to repair car brakes. Yet he was in a spiritual battle that he may not have even known he was in or had not figured out how to fight. He seems to have been struggling to find joy but probably didn't understand the biblical definition of joy as will be described in a future chapter. We believe that he listened to Satan's lies that told him he could never be good enough or to measure up to the standards he had set in his own life. I don't believe Nathan truly grasped the goodness of God's grace as described earlier in this book. I believe he was on a journey toward something he could never find because it was a dead-end journey that Satan deceived him into believing was true, but it was a lie.

*****

### Barbara

Very early on in our marriage, I realized I was a perfectionist. Although I lived a very full life as a young adult by being involved in my church and having a good job, I had lived at home until Mark and I married. I didn't realize it until we were in our own space and had opportunities of my own that I was a bit of a perfectionist. As a student and then an employee, it can be looked on as just having a good work ethic, which is highly acceptable and necessary. But a few months into our marriage, we were having friends in for supper. I made a pecan pie. Simple enough, except that it was about the second pie crust I made and the crust was far from perfect. As the pie baked, the imperfections (i.e., cracks) expanded. Pecan pie, being syrupy, leaked through the crust. I took a look at it, and I refused to serve it. Mark and I tried it the next day, and interestingly enough, it tasted fine—in fact, just like a pecan pie should! Almost instantly I realized how foolish I was and also that I had the tendencies of perfectionism. I also determined that I would not allow my life to be ruled that way. It may have been then that the truth in Philippians 1:6 took root, "Being confident of this, that He who began a good work in you will carry it on to completion until the day of Christ Jesus."

*****

I believe this is an example of how Satan can deceive anyone and in this case a believer. Perfectionism removes the power of God's grace in our lives as it allows us to trust in our abilities as opposed to the power of God. If you had asked us about perfectionism and Nathan before he died, we probably would have said that he had a great work ethic, but we didn't see his need or striving for perfection at that point. He was also very laidback in many ways, and I respected him for that and appreciated how his example encouraged me to "chill" at times. Again, I think now that this is another way that Satan deceived us as parents. So many people today are struggling with listening to Satan's lies, and they don't even identify where the struggle comes from, things like insecurity, depression, and anxiety, and yes, perfectionism. Some have become addicted to something—i.e., work, alcohol, drugs, shopping, etc.—to cover their pain; others are striving for joy, or peace, or comfort through their jobs or family or friends. They are in a spiritual war and have not identified it as such. I, too, have struggled with perfectionism. I didn't identify it until I was in my late thirties. I was working on a project with a friend, building an island for our kitchen. In the middle of the project my friend looked at me and said, "You're such a perfectionist." Of course, I disagreed with him and went home and told Barb what he had said about me. She shrugged her shoulders and said, "Yes, you are. Didn't you know that?" Ever since that incident, I have identified areas in my life where I am a perfectionist: in my preaching, in taking care of my car, and in other trivial things that really shouldn't matter that much. Sometimes my perfectionist personality has led to depressive days because in my own mind I had not lived up to my own expectations. It is a serious issue in the Christian life.

Second Corinthians 11:14 warns us that "Satan disguises himself as an angel of light." He will trick us into believing that the light we are following is the true light, and he does it so effectively that we are caught in his trap without even realizing it, like the proverbial frog in the kettle. We blindly continue pursuing his false light until it destroys our life. It happens to Christians and non-Christians alike. Non-Christians have no filter of discernment, but the Bible gives ample warning to Christians if we will look and listen.

In this chapter I will be exposing the war plan of Satan. We will be looking at what it means to be in a spiritual battle. After Nathan died, I was so angry at what the devil had done and what Nathan had allowed the devil to do that I went into a half-hour rant one evening in the privacy of my room. I never, ever talk to Satan, but that night I was so angry that I told him that although he thinks he got away with something and although he may have pulled the wool over Nathan's eyes, he just picked a fight with me and God. I told him that I would do everything in my power to expose his evil, deceptive darkness. I lectured him that he is a defeated foe and that a day is coming soon when he would be cast into outer darkness forever and that until that time I would warn people about his schemes, tell people about God's grace and forgiveness that will set them free from Satan's bondage, and that no stone would go unturned to expose his lies. I said so much more, but you get the idea. This chapter and other chapters to follow are my deliverance on that promise. Please read carefully, take it all in, underline, and look at the scriptures I share with you from the Bible, and then share it with others who are also being deceived by the enemy. We are at war, but we are fighting a defeated enemy. We need to make a choice to expose him for who he is.

The text I will be exploring is found in 1 Timothy 1:18–20. Dr. John MacArthur's writings and sermons on this subject have offered some tremendous insights that have helped me in understanding this text This is what the text says: "This charge I entrust to you, Timothy, my child, in accordance with the prophecies previously made about you, that by them you may wage the good warfare, holding faith and a good conscience. By rejecting this, some have made shipwreck of their faith, among whom are Hymenaeus and Alexander, whom I have handed over to Satan that they may learn not to blaspheme."

I am not an expert in the Greek language, but Dr. MacArthur says that the word *warfare* comes from a Greek word from which we get our word *strategy*. It means to fight as a soldier and to fight a noble campaign. In other words, the spiritual war we are in is not simply a skirmish and it is not simply a brief fight, but it is a long-term, continual campaign that Satan is using against us. The reason the apostle Paul wrote this letter to Timothy and the reason it has been passed down to us is to gear us up for fighting an excellent campaign. What Paul has in mind is not a human, physical war but a spiritual war that can affect us physically. As Paul wrote this letter to Timothy, he was aware that our spiritual enemy had infiltrated the church in Ephesus. Error was being taught in the church. False leaders were in positions of prominence and power and authority, and godliness was under attack. What Paul said to Timothy in these three verses is instructive to all of us because we are all engaged in the same spiritual campaign against us today. Maybe you are thinking of a church or an individual that is like the church in Ephesus when Paul wrote this letter, a church or a person under attack.

First, this war is primarily between God and Satan. It is a war between God and His truth and Satan and his lies. It is a war between God and His will and Satan and his will. Furthermore, it is a war that is not only fought between God and Satan but also between demons and holy angels, and between ungodly and godly men.

So the war begins at the level of God and Satan, but then it filters its way down to us. There are a number of elements involved in this war. In Luke 14 Jesus gave us an obvious principle that He applied to this subject in verse 31 when He said, "Or what king, going out to encounter another king in war, will not sit down first and deliberate whether he is able with ten thousand to meet him who comes against him with twenty thousand?" What Jesus is saying is that no king goes to war unless he understands the terms of battle. The king knows beforehand the power of his enemy, and he knows what is at stake when he goes into battle. I fear this is what has escaped the minds of so many modern-day believers today. So many people have bought into easy believism and cheap grace and the idea that Jesus is where you go to get all the goodies. They have missed the fact that we are in a spiritual battle and that life will not always be easy and that the stakes are high.

Where did this warfare originate? In the beginning of time, there was no war and there was no rebellion. Everything in God's universe and in the world were in perfect harmony with one another. Then there came a disastrous event that set God and Satan against one another for all eternity. We see it unfold for us in Ezekiel 28. Before we get to that prophecy, let me set the stage for you. Ezekiel is giving a prophecy against a place called Tyre. Tyre is a godless city we are introduced to in Ezekiel 26 and where God pronounced judgment on this city. It is located in the present-day Lebanon. Then in chapter 27, we read a kind of a funeral song about what is going to happen to Tyre. Reading further into chapter 28, in speaking against Tyre, Ezekiel goes beyond Tyre and its king and talks about the source of the king's antagonism against God. We learn that the king of Tyre is simply a pawn in the activity of Satan and that Satan is actually using the king to accomplish his purposes against God. We know from studying other Old Testament scriptures and Daniel's prophecy that Satan is behind all the godless nations of the world and that he and his demons are energizing a host of anti-God activities in the world. It was no different for Tyre. Although there was a king of Tyre, he was just a tool in the hand of the one behind the scenes, which really involves a warfare between God and Satan. We see this beginning in verse 11, "Moreover, the word of the Lord came to me." Ezekiel is referring to himself. He continues in verse 12, "Son of man, raise a lamentation over the king of Tyre." What follows in verse 12 could not be referring to a human being when he says, "Thus says the Lord God: 'You were the signet of perfection, full of wisdom and perfect in beauty.'" The word *signet* as translated in the ESV is referring to being sealed or being made complete. When you place a letter in an envelope, you seal the flap closed. It means to be consummated. In this passage the prophet is referring to Satan as having been given the seal of perfection, in that he was perfectly created by God. I don't know of any human being that we could say that of. Verse 12 goes on to say that Satan was "full of wisdom and perfect in beauty." You will never be able to say of a human being that he is full of wisdom or not lacking in wisdom and perfect in beauty.

Furthermore, verse 13a says, "You were in Eden, the garden of God." That statement cannot be referring to the king of Tyre, as he was not in the garden of Eden. Rather, the prophet is thinking about the serpent or the devil who was in the garden and tempted Adam and Eve. As an aside, this also means that the fall of Satan and the angels must have occurred sometime after the creation and occupation of the garden and sometime before Satan was turned into a serpent.

Here is something else I want you to see about our adversary, the devil. Verse 13c goes on to give a description of Satan's person as God created him. I feel the NKJV carries the clearest translation of this portion of scripture. "The workmanship of your timbrels and pipes was prepared for you on the day you were created." The NASB translates it as "The workmanship of your settings and sockets." The ESV translates it as "Your settings and your engravings." *Timbrels, settings* are small drums like those used to beat out the timing for a fife player. A fife is a small, high-pitched, transverse flute used primarily to accompany drums in a military or marching band. *Pipes, sockets* probably refer to tubes used to produce tones by blowing air through them, as in a pipe organ. I believe this is a reference to Satan's musical ability given to him by God. The *timbrels and pipes* are a reference to his vocal chords.

The prophet goes on to tell us why Satan may have needed these musical abilities in verse 14, "You were an anointed guardian cherub" (ESV). Let me help you to understand what that means. If you go to Ezekiel 10, we find a vision of the heavenly throne of God. It is a very strange picture of a wheel within a wheel. We also read of four cherubim standing at the four corners of the throne of God, and their job was to bring glory and praise to God. Satan was the "anointed guardian cherub." His job was to cover the mercy seat of atonement where sacrifice was made for the sin of man. He was the fifth cherub, which you don't see in Ezekiel 10 because he had already fallen. However, his job was a bit like a choir director, leading praises to God from the throne of God. Satan wasn't sent out to do other activities for God, but he was assigned to the throne room of God to bring praise to Him. The timbrels and pipes would have come in handy for this service to God.

Now when Satan fell from heaven, he did not lose his musical abilities. However, now he does not use them to bring glory to God, but rather to turn God's creatures against God. I believe his expertise in music can be seen in some of the music of our day as he influences people through certain music. You see, Satan knows his music and he hates the Lord, and that's a dangerous combination.

Also, notice verse 14 says, "I placed you; you were on the holy mountain of God" (ESV). That means that God created angels to fit into a ranking. So there are cherubim and seraphim. In addition, there are rulers and principalities and powers. Those are all terms of different positions or rankings in the hierarchy of the angels. Satan had been set as the supreme and anointed cherub. "In the midst of the stones of fire you walked" (verse 14c). Angels are not omnipresent like God is. They can be in only one place at a time. Satan's place was in the presence of God. Other angels could be absent from the presence of God doing other tasks for God, but not Satan. He was always with God. Verse 15a goes on to say, "You were blameless in your ways from the day you were created." Again, you cannot say that of any human being. He is emphasizing the absolute perfection of this creature. Then disaster strikes. Verse 15 continues, "till unrighteousness was found in you." Here we find the beginning of spiritual warfare as Satan pits himself against God. We are not certain how this happened because he lived in a perfect and sinless environment as a sinless and perfect creature. The only evidence we can find is found in verse 16, where it says, "In the abundance of your trade you were filled with violence in your midst, and you sinned." Somehow this angel became so enamoured with his own beauty and wisdom that pride built up inside of him and defiled him.

We find further evidence of the sin of Satan by going to Isaiah 14. Here again we find a prophecy indicating a greater power that is behind the scenes. This prophecy has to do with Babylon and its destruction. However, there was a greater power behind Babylon, in the same way there was a greater power behind Tyre. We find the power source in verse 12a, "How you have fallen from heaven, you star of the morning, son of the dawn!" (ESV). NKJV puts it this way: "How you are fallen from heaven, O Lucifer, son of the morning." The word *Lucifer* was not a direct Hebrew translation, but rather it is taken from the Latin. Lucifer is an accurate translation of *morning star* in Latin, but not if you are translating it from Hebrew. The word *Lucifer*, therefore, is not a proper name but is the Latin word for *morning star* or *day star*. It is probably a reference to the mortal Babylonian ruler. However, it seems to go beyond a description of a mortal king. If Jesus's reference in Luke 10:18, "I watched Satan fall from heaven like lightning," and John's in Revelation 19:1, "Then the fifth angel sounded, and I saw a star from heaven which had fallen to the earth," had this passage in mind, then there must be a secondary meaning to the passage. It seems to be referring to a Babylonian king and predicting his fall. Then Jesus and John used this text to indicate that Satan would fall. I recognize there is an argument for Isaiah 14 not being a description of Satan, and I could probably go on to give an argument on both sides. However, I am convinced this is a description of Satan.

To show how elevated this creature was, in Revelation 22:16, when God wanted to talk about the brilliance and magnificence of Christ, He calls Him "the bright and morning star." As I already indicated, here in Isaiah the name Lucifer in the Latin means "day star, son of morning." This shows us the marvelous glory of this creature. Then the prophet goes on to tell of the sin that rose up in his heart in verse 13, "But you said in your heart, 'I will ascend to heaven; I will raise my throne above the stars of God, And I will sit on the mount of assembly in the recesses of the north.'" Did you notice how many times the phrase *I will* is used? Clearly the sin was pride. Lucifer was so enamoured with his own beauty, and he was so close to God that he became jealous of God and wanted to be equal to God. It is the same sin that was found in the garden when Satan said to Adam and Eve in Genesis 3:5, "On the day you eat from it your eyes will be opened, and you will become like God, knowing good and evil." The very thing Lucifer wanted for himself is what he tempted Adam and Eve with. Isaiah 14:13 goes on to say, "But you said in your heart." Again, this sin is one that issues forth from the heart. It is invented by Lucifer. In essence, he said to himself, "It isn't enough for me where I am, but I want to go higher. I want to be at the very dwelling place of God and take my place with Him." Verse 13b continues, "I will ascend to heaven; I will raise my throne above the stars of God." The *stars* are the other angels. He is saying, "Even though I'm the leading angel, I will go beyond all the other angels." Verse 14 goes on to say, "I will ascend above the heights of the clouds." John MacArthur explains that in the Hebrew language the word *clouds* is singular and should be translated *cloud*. He is referring to the Shekinah glory of God. Lucifer was saying, "I am going to be above the height of God's glory." It is out of this self-generated sin that a spiritual warfare began.

God responded to this attack in verse 15 with a counter attack and says, "But you are brought down to Sheol, to the far reaches of the pit." Essentially God is saying that He would take Lucifer on and that He would devastate him.

Now you understand who Satan is and the nature of the supernatural conflict we are in. It is a conflict that is basically between God and Satan. It is not simply a little skirmish, but it is going on all the time, every single day, every day of the year. We can see the conflict in live action in the book of Job, where in chapter 1 Satan is described as wandering here and there in the earth. Then having appeared before the throne of God, he challenged God as to who Job would follow if God allowed everything to be taken away from him. First, this shows us that Satan is and will always be accountable to God and can do nothing without His permission. Second, it shows us that Satan is always trying to get one up on God, and in doing so he is attempting to diminish the power of God, the glory of God, the work of God, the purpose of God, and the will of God. This is the enemy we are up against today, and we need to take the battle seriously.

Maybe you are wondering how you fit into this conflict. If it is a conflict between God and Satan, then where do we as followers of Jesus Christ and humanity fit into the battle? First, Satan isn't alone in this conflict. It is in Revelation 12:3 where we read, "And another sign appeared in heaven: behold, a great red dragon, with seven heads and ten horns, and on his heads seven diadems." This verse is the summation of all forms of anti-God world governments. Satan is depicted as having ten horns because he is the supreme ruler of governments. So this is a description of Satan and how he embodies all the evil of the systems of man. Verse 4a goes on to say, "His tail swept down a third of the stars of heaven and cast them to the earth." When God cast Lucifer out of heaven, he took with him one-third of all the other angels of heaven. We don't know how many angels that entails, but they number more than we can count. The Bible talks about the angels in terms of ten thousand times ten thousand and thousands of thousands, which in the Greek language is the largest Greek word to express numeration. They do not have a word larger than ten thousand. It's like us saying, "Zillions and zillions." A third of them are actively involved with Satan. This tells us that Satan is not alone in this conflict. Two-thirds of the angels stayed loyal to God, and one-third defected with Satan. Furthermore, because the angels are not omnipresent, Satan does his dirty deeds in the world through these other evil angels who follow him. Now some of these evil angels aren't of any use to Satan because the book of Jude tells us that some of them are locked up in eternal chains. Therefore, although Satan started out with a third of the angels, some of them were put into chains.

We find the target of these fallen angels in Revelation 12. Verse 1 tells us, "And a great sign appeared in heaven: a woman clothed with the sun, with the moon under her feet, and on her head a crown of twelve stars." The woman referred to is Israel. The sun and the moon probably refer to Jacob and Rachel, and the twelve stars are the twelve sons of Israel. Verse 2 says the woman is with child. This is the Messiah, the Lord Jesus Christ. Let's pick up in verse 5, "She gave birth to a male child, one who is to rule all the nations with a rod of iron, but her child was caught up to God and to his throne." So Israel bears the child, and in the midst of the vision, in verses 3 to 4, we see Satan gathering his forces. At the end of verse 4 it says that he is ready to devour the child as soon as he was born. And in fact, that is exactly what happened in Bethlehem when Herod killed all the babies two years and under. Satan had been trying to destroy the Messiah all through history. He tried to destroy the godly line by corrupting an entire generation of people whom God had to drown in the flood. He tried to destroy the line of David by corrupting the nation of Israel so that there wouldn't be a seed. He tried to kill Christ through Herod. He tried to kill Christ by tempting him to fall to temptation in the wilderness. He tried to kill Christ in the garden and on the cross and by trying to keep Him in the grave. The dragon always fights against the Messiah, and he will fight against Christ when he comes in His return, and he will go on fighting until he is finally bound forever in the pit of hell.

In verse 7, we see that "war arose in heaven, Michael and his angels fighting against the dragon. And the dragon and his angels fought back." This is an all-consummating statement. There was a war in the past, there is a war going on in the present, and there will be war in the future. Furthermore, this war between Satan and God filters down to us. Verse 17 tells us, "Then the dragon became furious with the woman and went off to make war on the rest of her offspring, on those who keep the commandments of God and hold to the testimony of Jesus." Notice how the war started with God and Satan, then it went down through the holy angels and to the fallen angels, and now it is down to a warfare against those who know Jesus and keep the commandments of God. That's us, those who have made Jesus Savior and Lord of our lives. And yet Satan isn't particularly interested in us as individuals. Satan is targeting God. It is only in that we somehow have an impact in this world for the glory of God that Satan becomes interested in us as well. And it is because we stand with God that we are also at war with Satan. When we are defeated by him, there is a sense in which Satan has effectively attacked God. However, when we are victorious, there is a sense in which Satan has been defeated in his attack against God.

That means that when Satan attacks the church and its members get all out of sorts with one another and it gets a bad reputation in the community, Satan is really attacking God. When he attacks marriages by providing variants of what marriage is and by destroying what a real home is, Satan is really attacking God. When Satan attacks individual Christians and brings hardship and trouble and guilt and tragedy into their lives, depending on our response to the attack, God will either be glorified and Satan will be defeated, or God will be dishonored and we will have given a foothold to the enemy.

I have heard people make the statement "I don't even see a war going on." If you are able to say that, I am bold enough to stay that you have gone AWOL in your Christian faith and you are an un-courageous soldier because as Christians we expect hardship. We expect to be cut off from the affairs of this world because we are in a spiritual war. I have been a soldier in this war for many years now. I have seen battles break out in churches, I have seen leaderships get a big ego and think they know better than anyone else, including the anointed pastor. I have seen marriages broken because of self-righteous people who won't give in and say "I'm sorry," and I have personally experienced the effects of this warfare through disruptions in my own home during times when I've been preaching on certain topics. And now we have experienced the death of our own son, which we believe to be by the hand of Satan. The war rages on, and all of us are a part of the war.

Let me close this chapter by addressing how we can effectively fight this war. I will also address this topic more fully in a following chapter. The apostle Paul wrote in 2 Corinthians 10:4–6, "For the weapons of our warfare are not of the flesh but have divine power to destroy strongholds. We destroy arguments and every lofty opinion raised against the knowledge of God, and take every thought captive to obey Christ, being ready to punish every disobedience, when your obedience is complete." We cannot use our own intellect in this war. We cannot use our own wisdom or natural talents. Our weapons of warfare are not fleshly/carnal. Our weapons "have divine power to destroy strongholds." We can most definitely bring down the kingdom of Satan. Paul tells us in verse 5 to "take every thought captive to obey Christ." Our weapons of warfare are not mystical. They are not human intellect or in our ability or skill or ingenuity. Our weapons of warfare can be summed up in one thing, which is obedience to the Word of God. You see, the Word of God has power we do not have in ourselves. It is not found in a little formula, the right words to say, or some spiritual zap. Our spiritual warfare is nothing less than learning the life of obedience to the Word of God, and then by using the sword of the Word, we cut a swatch through the darkness. What God wants in this noble warfare is for us to live a life of obedience to Him.

I would like to end this chapter with the beautiful hymn written by Isaac Watts for us to consider as we engage in spiritual battle. The title of the song is "Am I a Soldier of the Cross?"

Am I a soldier of the cross, a follower of the Lamb?
And shall I fear to own His cause or blush to speak His
name?
Must I be carried to the skies on flower beds of ease
while others fought to win the prize and sailed
through bloody seas?
Are there no foes for me to face?
Must I not stem the flood?
Is this vile world a friend to grace to help me on to
God?
Sure I must fight if I would reign
Increase my courage, Lord. I'll bear the toil, endure
the pain, supported by Thy Word.

May this be your prayer as you fight the good fight for the glory
of God.

CHAPTER

# Fighting to Win

## 1 Timothy 1:18–20

In the previous chapter, we saw that all of us are in a spiritual war and that we are called to be in the battle. Our text is 1 Timothy 1:18, "Wage the good warfare." The entirety of the letter of 1 Timothy is dedicated to helping Timothy and us to know how to engage our enemy, the devil, in battle. In 1 Timothy 1:18, we are encouraged to engage in the battle, and at the end of the letter, we are reminded that we are in a war with Satan. Most Christians are dreadfully naive of the battle we are engaged in as followers of Christ. One time, a dear lady in one of my churches told me, "I don't like you preaching on Satan and spiritual warfare. I don't see Satan, and I don't feel like I'm in a battle." That lady is either not a Christian and not in the battle, or she is simply not aware of the battle that exists and is refusing to engage in it. Many people, however, are just like that lady. They may not say it out loud, but they don't believe in spiritual warfare, even though the evidence is right before their own eyes that it is occurring, sometimes in their own households. When a marriage is falling apart, that is evidence of spiritual warfare. When children are obstinate, disobedient, disrespectful, and eventually become prodigal children, that is evidence of spiritual warfare. Our son was engaged in a spiritual warfare he didn't know how to fight and that he probably didn't even identify in his own life, and I've made it my life mission to make sure that doesn't happen to anyone else.

As a pastor, most years I will preach a series of sermons on marriage and the family. This normally occurs between Mother's Day and Father's Day. It gives me a nice seven-message series. Our children were always good sleepers. However, during the preaching on marriage and the family, one of our sons would wake up on a Saturday night wailing, as if he had a bad nightmare. It took us a long time to calm him down. This went on each week during that series. One day I spoke with my associate pastor, a godly man ten years my senior. I shared with him what was going on and that it was so unusual. He said that this was nothing but an attack from the enemy and that we should pray against it. So we did. That week, and in the weeks to come, our son slept through the night again. However, this event, or some other disturbing event, would happen each year that I preached on marriage and the family. However, now we knew where it was coming from, so each year we began praying ahead of time that God would protect us from the attacks of the enemy. I wonder how many other people or families are under attack and they are not identifying it as such?

In the previous chapter, we were able to examine the nature of this warfare. We learned that as an extension of the battle between God and Satan that Satan will target followers of Christ in order to attack God Himself. The sooner we realize we are engaged in an intimate and personal conflict with the supernatural enemy of God, the sooner we can prioritize our lives. Paul said in Ephesians 6:12, "For we do not wrestle against flesh and blood, but against the rulers, against the authorities, against the cosmic powers over this present darkness, against the spiritual forces of evil in the heavenly places." All these terms are describing demons and their various rankings. We are engaged in a war with a supernatural enemy. No one understood that better than the apostle Paul, who, in his own testimony in 2 Corinthians 12:7, said, "So to keep me from becoming conceited because of the surpassing greatness of the revelations, a thorn was given me in the flesh, a messenger of Satan to harass me, to keep me from becoming conceited." We don't know specifically what the thorn given to Paul may have been, but he recognized it as coming from Satan, and he realized the intimacy of the attack. He also wrote in 1 Thessalonians 2:17–18, "But since we were torn away from you, brothers, for a short time, in person not in heart, we endeavored the more eagerly and with great desire to see you face to face because we wanted to come to you—I, Paul, again and again—but Satan hindered us." Again, Paul recognized the intimacy of Satan's attack by hindering him.

From the two previous verses, we can see how Satan can torment us with some kind of thorn in the flesh, and he can also stand in our way to hinder us, impede our way, and even detain us from doing God's work. Paul knew firsthand about this spiritual warfare, and in 1 Timothy 1, he calls Timothy to be aware of this spiritual battle and to engage in it. The way Paul calls Timothy to battle is by confronting false pastors, elders, and teachers in the church. It is because of my own experiences with spiritual warfare that I am also motivated to warn the reader today of the battle against your own life. In the following paragraphs, we will discover our responsibility and accountability in fighting this battle.

The assignment given to Timothy wasn't an easy one to fulfill, any more than it is for us today. However, there was an invading group of people in the church who were acting as agents of Satan and who were advocating for error through false doctrine and an ungodly lifestyle. This would be difficult for Timothy to confront because he wasn't having to confront workers down the chain of command, but he was confronting leaders of the church. Those leaders were attacking truth and doctrine and godliness.

First, they attacked the person of Christ. First Timothy 2:5–7 says, "For there is one God, and there is one mediator between God and men, the man Christ Jesus, who gave himself as a ransom for all, which is the testimony given at the proper time. For this I was appointed a preacher and an apostle (I am telling the truth, I am not lying), a teacher of the Gentiles in faith and truth." Apparently, there was some kind of an attack on the office of Christ as our mediator, on the sufficiency of Christ, and on the work of Christ. We see Paul addressing this again in 1 Timothy 3:16, "Great indeed, we confess, is the mystery of godliness: He was manifested in the flesh, vindicated by the Spirit, seen by angels, proclaimed among the nations, believed on in the world, taken up in glory." Paul is chronicling the life and work of Christ and seems to be saying, "Look, it's difficult to grasp, but God became flesh." We see this theme again in 1 Timothy 6:13–15, "I charge you in the presence of God, who gives life to all things, and of Christ Jesus, who in his testimony before Pontius Pilate made the good confession, to keep the commandment unstained and free from reproach until the appearing of our Lord Jesus Christ, which he will display at the proper time—he who is the blessed and only sovereign, the King of kings and Lord of lords." He is affirming and defending the deity of Christ and His sufficiency as mediator and the character of Christ that was under attack.

There was also an attack being mounted on the gospel of Christ. In 1 Timothy 1:14 he wrote, "Nor to devote themselves to myths and endless genealogies, which promote speculations rather than the stewardship from God that is by faith." The false teachers were espousing myths, fables, and genealogies that don't do anything but raise questions and don't bring any edification. Paul makes further comment in verse 5, "The aim of our charge is love that issues from a pure heart and a good conscience and a sincere faith." You see, they were turning aside and swerving from the true faith. Not only were they perverting the gospel, but also, they were perverting the law. We read in verse 7, "Desiring to be teachers of the law, without understanding either what they are saying or the things about which they make confident assertions." Here were teachers who really didn't have any idea about what they were saying or why they were saying it. It is as if they were just saying what made themselves feel good or what they thought the people wanted to hear, and they were all lies. Paul confronts this false teaching again in verse 15, "The saying is trustworthy and deserving of full acceptance, that Christ Jesus came into the world to save sinners, of whom I am the foremost." These false teachers may have been advocating a type of salvation for only the legalistic elite, only for people who could keep some kind of a standard they approved of. What Paul is saying is, "You want to think that only certain people can be saved. But look at me. I'm the chief of sinners, and Christ saved me." Further, in 1 Timothy 4:1 he proclaims, "Now the Spirit expressly says that in later times some will depart from the faith by devoting themselves to deceitful spirits and teachings of demons." In other words, not all teachers can be trusted. It could be that some teachers are actually inspired by the devil himself.

In the '90s there was a group of supposedly New Testament scholars who got together to vote on whether what Jesus said was really true. Really? Men are going to vote to determine if what Jesus said is true? To even suggest that we could do that is an attack on the credibility of the Word of God and on Christ Himself. However, people will do it because they are energized by Satan. In addition, remember that Satan's attack is against God and His church, and it comes through the mouth of false teachers. These people are not just well-meaning people who have slipped a little in their understanding, but they are actually agents of Satan. If we are to engage in the battle against evil, we must be vigilant to be on guard for such teachers and do whatever we can to root them out.

There was also an attack on the virtue of life and godly living. In 1 Timothy 1:5, Paul addresses some of these attackers when he said, "The aim of our charge is love that issues from a pure heart and a good conscience and a sincere faith." The false teachers didn't have those attributes. They didn't have integrity or character, a clear conscience, or a pure heart. Instead, they are as Paul states in verses 9 to 10, "Understanding this, that the law is not laid down for the just but for the lawless and disobedient, for the ungodly and sinners, for the unholy and profane, for those who strike their fathers and mothers, for murderers, the sexually immoral, men who practice homosexuality, enslavers, liars, perjurers, and whatever else is contrary to sound doctrine." Paul may be describing people who were in the church who were giving leadership. What an awful description he has given of them. Their morality matched their doctrine, and they had shipwrecked their faith. That's why Paul encourages us in 1 Timothy in 4:6–7, "If you put these things before the brothers, you will be a good servant of Christ Jesus, being trained in the words of the faith and of the good doctrine that you have followed. Have nothing to do with irreverent, silly myths. Rather train yourself for godliness."

The term *godliness* is a keyword in the Pastoral Epistles, and you can see how Paul addresses this idea throughout his letter. In chapter 5 he addresses the widows who had become lackluster and frivolous in their lifestyle. In chapter 6 he addresses teachers who had become proud and argumentative and perverse in disputing the truth. In chapter 3 you can see how Paul dealt with the qualifications for a leader in the church. He is to be blameless, the husband of one wife, temperate, sober-minded, etc. I haven't simply dropped into the text without a context, but I believe those qualifications are placed there as a contrast. There were all kinds of people in Ephesus who wanted to be a leader in the church. In chapter 1, verse 7 it says there were people who wanted to be teachers of the law. Chapter 3, verse 1 says there were people who wanted to be bishops. And Paul was saying to them, "You can't put them in those positions unless they have certain spiritual qualifications." I believe those qualifications are the contrasts to godly living I am speaking about. Paul said they are to be blameless rather than sinful and vile like the ones they had in office. They are to be one-woman men rather than men who are preoccupied with multiple women. They are to be temperate and sober-minded and have good behavior, as opposed to those they had in leadership. You see, they are all a contrast of behavior. When you get to chapter 5, verse 20, Paul says that if you find people who are not what they should be, they should be disciplined.

Timothy had a big job ahead of him. He needed to get rid of all the false teachers. He needed to call the people to rally around the truth of God's revelation and godly living. That's not an easy job for anyone. However, I do not believe it is any different from what we are dealing with in our own day. We may not be experiencing the exact same thing in our churches, but I can tell you that in Christianity around us, we are experiencing the same things as we are on the cutting edge of what Satan is trying to do to destroy the faith in people and the person of Christ. As we view our world today, we can easily see how Satan is attempting to destroy our confidence in the Lord's work to twist the message of the gospel, to lead people to tolerate evil and sin and any kind of lifestyle in the name of Christianity, to brainwash people to believe evil is good and that good is evil, and to destroy the real work of God. We are in a spiritual battle, and we need to be aware of it.

What do we need to understand in the fighting of this battle? It is the same as Timothy was instructed. We need to understand our responsibility and accountability. Paul said that Timothy had a responsibility to the church. In 1 Timothy 1:18 he said, "This charge I entrust to you, Timothy, my child, in accordance with the prophecies previously made about you, that by them you may wage the good warfare." The word *charge* refers to a military command. It is a word Paul uses at least four other times in this letter. It is not something to be discussed or to ponder over. Rather, Paul says that Timothy was under military obligation. He is commanding Timothy the same as a general would command a colonel. I love this story because it puts Timothy's responsibility in the category of duty. Not a lot of people today understand that word *duty*. It is not a word we talk a lot about, or that we understand a lot about today, except maybe in the context of a person who had joined a rank in the military. In Christianity we know about freedom, and we know about spiritual success, and we talk about joy and peace and fulfillment and satisfaction from a spiritual perspective, but we know very little about duty. It is something that has been built into our culture, and it has found its way into the church. The result is that there are many Christians whose personal preoccupation is solely self-indulgence. It's all about what makes them feel good. They will attend or leave a church based on whether they like the music or not, or on whether the preacher makes them feel good at the end of the service, or if he was entertaining enough. People are preoccupied with what does or does not govern their lives, but they don't know anything about duty.

I was watching a popular TV show about soldiers in a military unit who were on a mission that none of them really agreed with. One of the soldiers was having quite a bit of attitude about what they were called to do when his commanding officer said something like, "I don't care if you agree with it or not. It's your job, so just do your job." As followers of Christ, we don't always want to do or even like to do what we are called to do, but it is our duty. But what does that mean?

Let me try to illustrate this from a passage found in Luke 17. It is a passage that many of us just pass right over without giving it a lot of thought. This is what verses 7 to 10 say, "Will any one of you who has a servant plowing or keeping sheep say to him when he has come in from the field, 'Come at once and recline at table?' Will he not rather say to him, 'Prepare supper for me, and dress properly, and serve me while I eat and drink, and afterward you will eat and drink?' Does he thank the servant because he did what was commanded? So you also, when you have done all that you were commanded, say, 'We are unworthy servants; we have only done what was our duty.'" The servant says, "Don't give me an honorary degree. Don't hail me as a hero. I just did my duty." What has happened in our day to just doing our duty as Christians? As a pastor of nearly forty years I have seen how we have entered a generation of people who like to whine about how the church isn't meeting their needs, how we talk too much about the end times, that we don't sing songs they like, about how old-fashioned the church is, and that because we don't meet their needs they have decided to stay away from church. Their response ought to be to get involved and take some responsibility to see change made, but instead, they are saying, "You change, and we'll consider coming back." However, as Christians, we are duty bound to do the work of ministry as a priest in the church, even if it is hard and we don't like it.

We have a duty, but we also have a commission. It is in 1 Timothy 1:18 that Paul says, "This charge I entrust to you." The word *entrust* is a word that talks about a deposit you put in the bank. Paul gave Timothy a valuable deposit, which is the deposit of truth, more valuable than anything is. We see it again in 2 Timothy 2:2, "And what you have heard from me in the presence of many witnesses entrust to faithful men, who will be able to teach others also." Paul is saying, "Timothy, I entrusted this truth to you, now keep it and entrust it to others." He repeatedly told Timothy to take care of this sacred trust. The lesson for us today is to watch out for people who have some new doctrine or some new teaching that goes outside the parameters of Scripture because the deposit Paul gave to Timothy has been passed down to us, and when you hear about some theology that no one has ever heard of before, run the other direction.

We have an ancient trust to be preserved, and Satan is always trying to pollute it by watering it down, by causing us to question it, or by attempting to make us think it really doesn't mean what it says. We have an accountability and a commission to the church to keep.

We also have an accountability to the Lord. In 1 Timothy 1:19 Paul tells us, "Holding faith and a good conscience. By rejecting this, some have made shipwreck of their faith." Having faith means believing in the truth. It means to have a commitment to believing the truth of God, to hold to the faith, and not let it go, no matter what.

Throughout this epistle, Paul has been talking about those who were in error concerning the faith. However, he says that if we are to fight the good fight against our enemy, then we cannot abandon the truth of God because that is precisely what Satan wants us to do. This is his plan in his battle against God and His kingdom.

We are also called on to have a good conscience. A good conscience simply means a conscience that is pure and undefiled. Your conscience is the self-judging faculty that tells you that your life is in order or that it needs a tune-up. In my car, when it is time for an oil change or a need to take it to a mechanic for service, a light will come on my dashboard. It is a warning sign that everything may not be all right. Our human conscience does the same thing for us. It's what Paul is talking about in Acts 24:16, where he said, "So I always take pains to have a clear conscience toward both God and man." To have a clear conscience means everything is all right. No warning signs are lighting up.

Our obligation to God is to hold to the truth and to live a pure life. We are called to be sound in truth and in doctrine. Theological error has its roots in moral rather than intellectual soil. That means that when people teach false doctrine, it isn't that they don't understand, but it's that they have a theology that accommodates their evil nature. Don't think for a minute that false teachers, liberals, cultists, or anyone else who teaches false doctrine are just poor, well-meaning, nice people who have gone astray. No, they are in error because their heart is fueled by Satan and they are evil. Furthermore, they won't submit their evil heart to the cleansing work of Christ. And the reason some so-called theologians come together to vote on what Jesus said isn't because they cannot know the truth of the Bible, but it is because there are things in the Bible they will not submit to. In order to avoid unnecessary submission, they just get rid of any teaching of Jesus they don't like or don't agree with. That comes from the pit of hell itself.

Our call as faithful soldiers in God's army is to understand our responsibility and accountability to the church and to God. Furthermore, we have a responsibility to deal with our enemies, and I will deal with that in the next chapter. But right now I would like to challenge you that if you desire to win this battle between God and Satan, your part is to be aware of the battle, to fight tooth and nail for the truth, and to live a pure life. Also, when we find error being taught, we need to confront it and fight alongside our Savior to bring the truth.

If you are reading this book and you have never received Christ as your Savior, I need you to know that the devil is fighting on your behalf to keep you from knowing Jesus by blinding your eyes to the truth. By your refusing to accept Christ as Lord and Savior, you have essentially chosen the side of Satan. I pray you will submit to Christ and let Him deliver you from sin and bondage to Satan.

If you are a follower of Christ, I understand the task we are called to is a high calling and is not an easy one to attain. However, Christ would never call us to a task we are not able to accomplish and that He will not give support to through the Spirit who dwells in us. Second Timothy 1:7 says, "For God gave us a spirit not of fear but of power and love and self-control." In other words, we can do this, but only as we depend on the spirit of God who gives the ability.

CHAPTER

# Delivered to Satan (Part 1)

## 1 Timothy 1:18–20

These few chapters have been dedicated to the task of exposing the darkness and how Satan is involved in or how he wants to be involved in the affairs of our lives. I have heard of few, if any, preachers address this issue extensively, except perhaps by a perfunctory statement of some sort in a sermon here or there, but not enough to actually warn people of the battle we, as followers of Christ, are engaged in on a daily basis. This chapter and the next couple of chapters will be difficult for you to read, and they are difficult for me to write as I have seen firsthand what giving in to the enemy can do to a person. Let's remember that Satan's only function in this world is to kill, steal, and destroy. His greatest desire is to keep people from knowing Christ as Savior. He wants more than anything to steal any joy we can experience in the Lord, and he wishes to destroy our lives. I believe with all my heart that Satan stole Nathan's joy and he was able to kill him, but Satan could not destroy him or his relationship with Christ. I dealt with that topic in chapters 2 and 3. I believe there will be many who will accept this teaching because it is founded in the Word of God, but it will be difficult to hear because it is difficult to believe this happens in our world and in our lives, and we want to believe something else. I can honestly say that before Nathan's death, I believed in spiritual warfare, but I never understood it to the depth of what I understand it now, having experienced the greatest of losses as a result of this battle. On the other hand, there will be some who will outright reject this teaching because they don't want to believe what God says is true. Some people would rather believe in some fairy tale about the devil and that it is a story that doesn't really affect them. The lady I described in the last chapter fits into this category. Be that as it may, I am compelled by the Lord to teach the truth of the Word of God. I didn't want to write these chapters and I had not just a few conversations with God about it, but He won; so I must write. I must shine light into the darkness that has entrapped so many.

In this chapter and the next two, I will be talking about what it means to be delivered to Satan. Paul wrote in 1 Timothy 1:18–20, "This charge I entrust to you, Timothy, my child, in accordance with the prophecies previously made about you, that by them you may wage the good warfare, holding faith and a good conscience. By rejecting this, some have made shipwreck of their faith, among whom are Hymenaeus and Alexander, whom I have handed over to Satan that they may learn not to blaspheme." The word *delivered* or *handed over* in verse 20 means to remove protection. It means to be given over to and exposed to great danger. It is a bit like when we teach our children how to ride a bicycle. We begin by putting training wheels on their bike, and those wheels provide a certain degree of protection from them falling over. Besides, we are standing there to catch them if something happens. Eventually we take off the training wheels and we run along behind them with our hand on the seat of the bike. About the time we think they have their balance, we let go and step away. In essence, we have delivered them over to the bike and to their own ability to balance it, and we have exposed them to all sorts of danger—the mailbox, the tree or the hedge, to falling over and breaking an arm. The idea is that we take our hands completely off and we let them go. This is what Paul is describing when he uses the phrase *handed over to Satan.* He is saying that those people are removed from under the protection of God and the protective umbrella of the church.

Let me describe for you whom this directive applies to. In 1 John 5:19, we read, "We know that we are from God, and the whole world lies in the power of the evil one." From that verse we discover that in one sense the world is already in the hands of Satan because it was delivered to him through sin. Therefore, to turn someone over to Satan means that they were not at that time fully in Satan's control. So Paul must be talking about someone who finds themselves under the umbrella of protection provided by the church and or a Christian family. How many people realize that simply by being a part of a local church they come under the protection and care of God, whether they are a believer or nonbeliever? It is the splash affect. If you are not a follower of Christ, by simply being in the proximity with the redeemed community of God, you receive a certain amount of protection and blessing from God. The same is true of an unbeliever who is married to a believer. However, to be delivered to Satan means to be taken out from under that protection and left fully exposed to Satan.

An illustration will help us to understand this concept. In Genesis 18, we read the story of how God dealt with Sodom and Gomorrah, and I think you'll see some startling things as we look at the story from fresh eyes. The story begins with a conversation between Abraham and God. God told Abraham He was going to destroy the city of Sodom because of its great sin. Verse 26, "And the Lord said, 'If I find at Sodom fifty righteous in the city, I will spare the whole place for their sake.'" Now that's pretty amazing. Here is an entire city that has such horrible sin in it that God wants to destroy it. Yet for the sake of fifty righteous people in the city, He would spare it. These cities have actually been located through archeological digs in Israel. Some say there could have been as many as a couple of million people living there, and for the sake of fifty people God would spare it. Here we can see the insulation that comes to the undeserving simply because of their proximity to the righteous.

As the account goes on in the Scripture, Abraham begins bargaining with God, and he eventually whittles the number down to ten righteous people. God said to him in verse 32, "For the sake of ten I will not destroy it." That's amazing. There is an entire area of thousands of people who would be spared for the sake of ten people. By the way, God didn't find ten righteous people in Sodom, and

He did destroy the city, which has been discovered and confirmed through archeological digs in the area. The point I am making, however, is that a proximity to and involvement with the redeemed people of God acts as an insulation and a protection, even to unbelievers. This is also true today in the church of Jesus Christ. Of course, there are people who attend certain churches and are involved in churches who are not followers of Jesus Christ. However, simply through their association, they get a certain amount of protection and blessing along with the believers.

We also see these principles illustrated in 1 Corinthians 7. In this chapter Paul is addressing the question of whether a believing marriage partner should stay married with an unbelieving partner. He answers the question in verse 14, "For the unbelieving husband is made holy because of his wife, and the unbelieving wife is made holy because of her husband. Otherwise your children would be unclean, but as it is, they are holy." In other words, an unbelieving spouse and children within a family, where there is a believer present, are all under the umbrella of God's blessings. The word *holy*—other translations use the word *sanctified*—is not a reference to salvation, but it means that there is a splash affect. They are around when the showers of blessing come, and they get wet. What I am saying is that there is a shelter for those who don't know God under the umbrella of the believer. We see this splash effect in both the Old and New Testaments.

To sum it up, this means that to be delivered over to Satan is the action of taking someone out from under the insulation and protection of the believing community and exposing them to the full blast of Satan's power. It is the idea of God withdrawing His hand of protection in whatever degree of blessing that person has been enjoying.

Let me show you some examples of people who had been delivered over to Satan. In this chapter, I will look exclusively at people who are believers who were allowed to be exposed to Satan's fury. Some people will say there are no conditions under which any Christian should ever be subject to Satan, but I disagree. In the Scriptures we find examples when God personally put people out from under the protection of His hand and into Satan's control.

Let's begin by thinking of the story of the Old Testament character Job. In Job 1, we are introduced to a man who was perfect and upright and who feared God and shunned evil. He had ten children, seven thousand sheep, three thousand camels, five hundred yokes of oxen, and a great household. He was not only a godly man, but he was extremely blessed by God. In fact, Job was the greatest of all the men in the East.

Job's sons held a great feast in their houses, and they sent for their three sisters to eat and drink with them. Job 1:5 tells us, "And when the days of the feast had run their course, Job would send and consecrate them, and he would rise early in the morning and offer burnt offerings according to the number of them all. For Job said, 'It may be that my children have sinned and cursed God in their hearts.' Thus Job did continually." We don't have any reason to believe that Job's children did sin or curse God, but Job wasn't taking any chances. This is the picture of a good and godly man and the most prosperous man in the East.

Now look what happens in verse 6, "Now there was a day when the sons of God came to present themselves before the Lord, and Satan also came among them." We don't know why Satan was before the throne of God with all the other angels, but this shows us that all the created angels, including fallen angels, are subject to and are required to answer to God. On this occasion, God asked Satan in verse 7, "From where have you come?" To which Satan answered, "From going to and fro on the earth, and from walking up and down on it." This tells us where Satan spends his time. The Lord continued in verse 8, "Have you considered my servant Job, that there is none like him on the earth, a blameless and upright man, who fears God and turns away from evil?" You see, Satan is always attempting to diminish the work of God. He wants to destroy the work of God and show Him up, and I am pretty sure Satan was at the throne of God to make some sort of accusation against God before all the other angels. He wanted to make God look bad. That is his nature. However, God asked him, "Have you considered my servant Job and what a good man he is?" Satan answered Him in verses 9 to 10, "Does Job fear God for no reason? Have you not put a hedge around him and his house and all that he has, on every side? You have blessed the work of his hands, and his possessions have increased in the land." Satan was accusing Job of worshiping God simply because God was dumping all those good things in his lap. Furthermore, he accused God of putting a hedge of protection around him and his house and around everything he owned. So he asked the question, "Why do you think he worships you?" And Satan's answer was because Job knows who delivers the goods. Satan continued in verse 11, "But stretch out your hand and touch all that he has, and he will curse you to your face." God responded in verse 11, "Behold, all that he has is in your hand."

I know it is hard to imagine, but God just turned Job over to Satan, which was a divine act by a sovereign God. Therefore, Satan went out and totally obliterated all that Job had. He killed his sons and daughters (verse 19). He infused hatred in the hearts of the Sabeans who went and killed some of his animals. He got some people to start a fire, and they burned up all his crops and all his sheep. Then he motivated the Chaldeans and others, and they stole all his camels and killed his servants. Everything Job owned was gone in one fell sweep. He was completely reduced to nothing. Job tore his robe and shaved his head and fell on the ground and cursed God. Wait! Is that what he did? No, he didn't curse God, but verses 20 to 22 tell us, "Then Job arose and tore his robe and shaved his head and fell on the ground and worshiped. And he said, 'Naked I came from my mother's womb, and naked shall I return. The Lord gave, and the Lord has taken away; blessed be the name of the Lord.' In all this Job did not sin or charge God with wrong." At this point we might think, "So, what's the point of it all?" The devil thought the only reason Job followed God was because God blessed him, and the lesson is that God made a point to the devil and to the whole world and everyone who reads this story that true saving faith is not dependent on positive circumstances. It is as though God is saying, "When I redeem a life and when I transform a life and when a person truly loves me, that love is not built on circumstances." In a sense, Job is redundant to the story because God is making a point to Satan, and to make the point He used Job. In fact, the whole theme of Job is not simply to teach us about how to deal with suffering, but it is to show us the character of a godly person. Job loved and worshiped God, not because of what God gave to him, but out of pure devotion alone.

You probably know the rest of the story. Satan came back in chapter 2, and God gave him another crack at Job in verse 6, "And the Lord said to Satan, 'Behold, he is in your hand; only spare his life.'" Satan left the presence of God and inflicted Job with boils and sores from head to foot. That shows us that Satan can bring diseases on us. Job went out and sat on an ash pile scraping scabs off his body when along came his wife who said, "Do you still hold fast your integrity? Curse God and die" (verse 9). Job shows his character when he replied to her in verse 10, "You speak as one of the foolish women would speak. Shall we receive good from God, and shall we not receive evil?" In all this Job did not sin with his lips. This is absolutely incredible. God is making a huge point about the nature of true salvation and godliness. We might think it isn't very fair to make Job into an illustration to make His case, yet we need to be able to look beyond the life of this one individual to see that God was making a point for all eternity and that He has the sovereign right to do that.

Job couldn't explain what was happening to him. He didn't have the book to read. However, throughout the book, Job is asking questions and complaining and challenging God about what was happening to him, and the heavens are silent. In fact, we don't know that Job ever knew why all this happened to him because this was happening in heaven.

In some ways, I can sympathize with Job in my own journey as we grieve the life of Nathan. We believe he was in a spiritual battle that was happening in the heavenly realms and that it was a battle we won't fully understand until eternity. I am not holding Nathan up to the stature of the likes of a Job, but I am saying that a spiritual battle is taking place in the heavens that none of us can see, and for reasons unknown to us, God allows Satan to take this battle to the realms of His children. I believe that in one way or another, every child of God is facing spiritual battles to some degree in their life. They may be little skirmishes, or they may be all-out wars. Some of these battles we shrug off as consequences of life, coincidences, or just things that happen. I'm not saying that Satan is behind every bad event that happens in life, but I'm asking that you be alert to the fact that it may be an attack from the enemy.

Finally, God speaks to Job in chapter 38. In verse 1 it says, "Then the Lord answered Job out of the whirlwind and said." Do you know what the Lord said? He didn't say, "Job, let me tell you all about what has happened to you." No, Job didn't know what was happening, and God never told him. Rather, the Lord comes and says to Job in verse 4, "Where were you when I laid the foundation of the earth? Tell me, if you have understanding." God goes on to tell Job about all His creative acts and basically says to him, "I'll do what I want to do, and who are you to question it?" Job gets the message, and in chapter 42:2, he answers the Lord by saying, "I know that you can do all things, and that no purpose of yours can be thwarted." He is saying to God, "You're sovereign and you can do anything. I am a fool for opening my mouth, and I apologize." And this dear godly man repents before God.

The whole point of the story of Job is to show us the character and the genuine godliness of this man. It is designed to show us the unbreakable reality of a redeemed person who refused to abandon God, no matter what. As a result, Job learned a deeper love of God. He found some sins in himself that he didn't know about. And he learned what it means to submit to a divine rule, even if he didn't understand.

Furthermore, we see an example of how a believer can be turned over to Satan, but Satan will always have limits as to how far he can go. Therefore, let's not be surprised when, even in the confines of the church, there are some members who have things happen to them that we can't find any reasons to explain. At those times we might feel like God has totally removed His hand from us and we may feel confused with so many questions unanswered, yet the answer is somewhere on a divine level and it may never be revealed to us. Be assured, however, that God has a divine and holy purpose, and it is in His grace we believe there will be a time of restoration and great blessing. We just need to leave that in God's hands.

In Job's case, because he passed the test, God poured out His blessing on him. Job 42:12 says, "And the Lord blessed the latter days of Job more than his beginning. And he had 14,000 sheep, 6,000 camels, 1,000 yoke of oxen, and 1,000 female donkeys." God gave back to him all his crops and animals. And verse 13 says that God gave him seven more sons and three of the most beautiful daughters in all the land.

I believe there comes a time in all our lives when, if we continue to be faithful and we pass the test, God will grant a reward. The reward may not be in this lifetime. I'm pretty sure that Barb and I won't get a replacement for Nathan. But for a time, in God's sovereign purpose, He may choose to turn one of His own over to Satan, and it may be for no other purpose than to demonstrate to a watching world the strength and character of genuine conversion so that the world will see people who don't love God simply for what He gives to them, but for who He is. I pray that will be my testimony to the world.

In our world today, it seems to me that our weak, wishy-washy, shallow, pop theology is completely ignorant of these truths. You see, God used Job to prove the character of true love and devotion to God, and this in turn brings greater glory to God.

In the next chapter, I will take you to the New Testament to see more illustrations of this principle, but before we go there, I want to make sure you get the whole point of Job and his suffering. We need to ask ourselves the question "Is God getting the glory through the suffering I am going through?" That's a question I continually ask myself. You see, we may never know for sure why certain events happen in our lives—at least not until we reach heaven, but we must remember that we do not love God just for the good things He does for us, but we must love Him for who He is. Let's let our love for Him grow stronger as we realize that God is always in control and has a divine purpose for everything.

CHAPTER

# Delivered to Satan (Part 2)

## 1 Timothy 1:18–20

In the previous chapter we began by discovering what it means to be delivered to Satan by looking at a couple of Old Testament examples. Again, this teaching is difficult for some people to hear, and they will reject it outright with no consideration. This is because they either don't see Satan as a personal and active living being and simply think of him as a fairy-tale figure in red tights. Or they do not think Satan could ever touch them personally, so why think about him at all? Or perhaps the reason they reject this teaching is because they do not consider the Bible to be truthful on the matter.

For those who are still interested (you are believers, and you are still reading), in the last chapter we saw from 1 John 5:19 that "the whole world lies in the power of the evil one." In other words, the world was delivered over to Satan through sin, which means that whatever happens in this world that does not reflect the nature of God must be the result of Satan's activity in the world. Otherwise, why do people go on killing sprees? Why do parents abuse a child? Why do we have laws being passed that are anti-Christian value in nature? Why is there such rampant exposure of sexual abuse? Why on earth does a person decide to take his/her own life? Sure, we could pass these things off as mental health-related, environmental behavior, and a plethora of other excuses for such behavior. Some people tried to excuse Nathan's suicide on a mental disorder, without any evidence. One person said they read an article about schizophrenia and that maybe Nathan was schizophrenic However, from a biblical perspective, these are all behaviors that are a result of Satan's influence and activity in our world. His ultimate goal is to attack the throne of God, and the only way he can do that is by attacking God's world and God's people. And by the way, I am not saying there is no mental illness in the world that causes bad behavior, but I am saying that Satan will use all of this for his purposes.

Now Paul tells Timothy in 1 Timothy 1:20, "Hymenaeus and Alexander, whom I have handed over to Satan that they may learn not to blaspheme." From the previous chapter, we learned that to be "handed over to Satan" means to abandon to or to remove protection from. While Nathan was living under our roof at home, he fell under our protection as a spiritual home. However, a month before he took his life he had moved to another town. This particular town is known to have a demonic coven of Satan worshipers who are constantly praying against the church and God's people. In fact, this particular town has had a very high rate of suicide cases in it, to such an alarming rate that a group of Christians and pastors hold twenty-four-hour prayer meetings to combat it and the public schools have on occasion invited pastors to come to their schools to speak to the students about the subject. This is the town Nathan moved to, out from under our protection, and was attacked by the enemy. Regrettably, even having studied two years in Bible school and attending church his entire life, he was not equipped to do battle. I am determined to do whatever I can, not to allow this same thing to happen to anyone else.

To be *turned over* to Satan means to be removed from the protection of God and exposed to the full force of Satan's power. In the last chapter we learned that God Himself exposed His servant Job to Satan's power. We learned that the book of Job is not just a book teaching us how to handle trials when they come our way, but God was using Job as an illustration to the world and to us of a person who is truly saved and truly committed to God. A true believer does not love God just because of the stuff God can give him, but he loves God for who He is. Many times, the answers to our trials in life lie somewhere on a divine level that might never have been revealed to us, but we can trust that God has a plan and a purpose in it all.

In this chapter I want to go to the New Testament for examples of people being handed over to Satan. First, we find how Jesus Himself was delivered to Satan. Jesus is even more upright than Job, being God in the flesh, utterly and absolutely without sin. However, in Matthew 4:1, we read, "Then Jesus was led up by the Spirit into the wilderness to be tempted by the devil." Notice that Jesus was led to the wilderness by the Spirit. Mark 1:12 puts it this way, "The Spirit immediately drove him out into the wilderness." The purpose for driving Jesus into the wilderness was for Him to be tempted by the devil. It might be difficult to believe, but God not only turned Job over to the devil, but He also turned Christ over to the devil. In the same way that God placed Job into Satan's hands and proved the character of true salvation and proved Job's character, God turned Christ over to the devil. Through His temptations Christ showed that He would not break or waver, and He would stand true as the perfect God-man. The temptation of Jesus went on for forty days and nights. I believe the temptations probably came at the end of the forty days when Jesus was at His weakest state physically due to the lack of food and water. However, if you compare all the gospel records, you will find that there was temptation from the devil throughout the forty days.

I don't know if you have ever fasted (ceased to eat food) for a period of time, but most people can't seem to go for even a few hours without food and maybe some food in-between as well. Most studies say that to be sustainable you can survive only around twenty-one to thirty-two days without food. Ghandi went on a hunger strike and went twenty-one days without food, with just sips of water. There are only a few extreme cases where someone has lasted up to fifty days. After a few weeks, your body essentially starts to shut down. However, we are told that Jesus fasted forty days and nights. Therefore, when the devil came to Him, He was at a very vulnerable state and extremely weak. On that note, one of the Puritans once said that "Satan is a pirate who looks to find a vessel that sails without a fleet." You see, Satan is always looking to find some believer who is isolated and alone and without the protection of others. That is why it is so dangerous to come out from under the umbrella protection of the church because it is then that you are most vulnerable. In the previous chapter, I talked about how the church and a Christian home provides a canopy of protection from the enemy to those who find themselves under it, both believers and nonbelievers alike. For unbelievers, that does not mean they are automatically saved from their sins, simply because they find themselves in a place of protection. However, we're talking about the splash effect of the blessings that come to the believer. So here was Christ, alone for forty days and nights, out from under the protection of God and other believers. He was weak, in a place of barrenness, on a cliff overlooking the Dead Sea. I have visited that location, and it isn't a place you would want to camp out in for very long. It was there that the devil came to Him by design from God who led Him there by the Spirit and tempted Him to do evil.

Let's examine the temptations given to Jesus. In Matthew 4:3 Satan tempted Jesus to make some bread to eat. "And the tempter came and said to him, 'If you are the Son of God, command these stones to become loaves of bread.'" *If* you are the Son of God? That is exactly who He is. But the temptation was to use the fact of Jesus's deity against Him. Didn't the Son of God have the right to eat? Didn't the Son of God make everything that was made? Furthermore, if Jesus could make bread for a multitude, which He in fact did later on in His ministry, then couldn't Jesus also make some for Himself? Do you see how Satan is appealing to Jesus's right to have what He deserved? Satan is doing the same thing in people's lives in our world today. Everyone is demanding his or her rights. Some of those demands are legitimate and long overdue, and some of the demands are nothing but Satan-enticed temptations, desiring things just to satisfy the lust of the flesh.

Secondly, Satan tempted Jesus to take a dive off the pinnacle of the temple. Matthew 4:5–6 says, "Then the devil took him to the holy city and set him on the pinnacle of the temple and said to him, 'If you are the Son of God, throw yourself down, for it is written, "He will command his angels concerning you," and "On their hands they will bear you up, lest you strike your foot against a stone.'" The temptation was that if Jesus pulled off this stunt with nothing happening to Him, then people would celebrate Him as the Messiah. Satan knows the Bible, and he took his quote from Psalm 91:11–12, which is a promise of protection for those who trust in God. Yet Jesus's response to the devil uncovered his motivation when He said, "On the other hand, it is written: 'You shall not put the Lord your God to the test.'" Besides, Jesus didn't need to prove who He was. He knew He was the Messiah whether anyone else believed it or not.

Then the devil tempted Jesus to take the kingdoms of the world. Matthew 4:8–9 says, "Again, the devil took him to a very high mountain and showed him all the kingdoms of the world and their glory. And he said to him, 'All these I will give you, if you will fall down and worship me.'" Again, you can see how Satan is trying to usurp the position of God, in that the kingdoms already belong to Jesus. The devil was tempting Jesus to prematurely take what would eventually be His anyway. He was goading Christ to act in His own timing instead of waiting for God the Father's plan to be fulfilled.

You see, the devil tempted Jesus in areas where He had a right, yet even in His weakness and aloneness Christ resisted. Finally, verse 11 says, "Then the devil left him, and behold, angels came and were ministering to him." Jesus had passed the test, and after forty days and nights of fasting and refusing each of the devil's three enormous temptations, Jesus gave evidence that, though He was fully human and subject to temptation, He remained sinless. Then God sent angels to minister to Jesus, likely involving food and water.

The lesson in all this is that God put His own Son in the hands of Satan, and then God blessed Jesus with the ministry of angels for passing the test, in the same way He blessed Job for passing the test. So we see that by His own sovereign design, God may choose to put one of His own, even His own Son into the hands of Satan. The reason is always to bring greater glory to His name.

Another example in the Scriptures is the apostle Paul being delivered to Satan. I dealt with this in a previous chapter, but it bears mentioning again with some further lessons to learn. In 2 Corinthians 12:1 Paul wrote, "I must go on boasting. Though there is nothing to be gained by it, I will go on to visions and revelations of the Lord." Paul had so many visions and revelations from the Lord. He said in verse 2, "I know a man in Christ who fourteen years ago was caught up to the third heaven—whether in the body or out of the body I do not know, God knows." Paul was talking in second person about himself because he didn't want to sound like he was boasting, but he said that there was a time when he had been caught up to the third heaven. He was talking about the dwelling place of God. In verse 3 he said he had been caught up into paradise, but he didn't know whether it was in the body or out of the body. He didn't know the actual spiritual dynamics of his experience, only that he knew that he was there. He continued sharing his experience in verse 4 by saying, "And he heard things that cannot be told, which man may not utter." God didn't even allow him to talk about the whole experience. Then he said in verse 5, "On behalf of this man I will boast, but on my own behalf I will not boast, except of my weaknesses" As you can imagine, there would have been a huge temptation for Paul to boast about all his successes and visions and revelations and his experience in heaven.

Today, people would write books, go on speaking tours, and maybe make a movie about their experience. Not Paul. He said, "I'm not going to do that. In fact, I think I'll just boast about my weaknesses." Further, Paul said in verse 6, "Though if I should wish to boast, I would not be a fool, for I would be speaking the truth; but I refrain from it, so that no one may think more of me than he sees in me or hears from me." In other words, he is saying that he didn't want anyone to have an unfair or exaggerated opinion of him. Then he added in verse 7, "So to keep me from becoming conceited because of the surpassing greatness of the revelations, a thorn was given me in the flesh, a messenger of Satan to harass me, to keep me from becoming conceited." What kept Paul from boasting about himself and in all the experiences and revelations he had was some kind of physical affliction he calls a *thorn*. Imagine this godly man who was upright like Job, this man who dealt with sin in his life by keeping short accounts with God, a man who had had an experience of heaven, yet God allowed Satan to buffet him with some kind of irritating, debilitating *thorn* in his flesh. I believe this text is telling us that God turned Paul over to Satan to inflict him. The affliction was not the work of God but the work of Satan. God allowed the devil to do it to keep Paul weak so that he would be dependent on God.

You see, people who have great gifts tend to need this kind of buffeting because it is easy for them to become self-dependent instead of leaning on God. Oswald Chambers said, "Before God can use a man greatly, He must wound him deeply." Chambers went on to say, "If we are ever going to be made into wine, we will have to be crushed—you cannot drink grapes. Grapes become wine only when they have been squeezed." Most people enjoy grape juice and some people enjoy wine, but symbolically few people enjoy the squeezing process, which is what is required for us to be of full value to God.

I would have never chosen to lose my son to suicide. Who would ever chose such a thing? In fact, when we were having our children I remember thinking to myself that I could never imagine losing one of our children to death. I felt like it would absolutely break me. Yet the very thing I feared the most is what God has allowed to happen, and I'm still here to tell you about it. Not because I am so strong or courageous or even so spiritual, but because God has been leading me and ministering to me day by day, year by year, as I deal with my great loss. It hasn't been easy. I still blame myself at times, that maybe I missed something or that I wasn't more in tune with Nathan or that I should have pushed when he became silent. But through all of it, I am reminded of my need to pursue God with all my might because without His power to sustain me I would crumble. Furthermore, I am not the same person I was in 2017. I have greater compassion for others who are going through tragedy in their lives. I have a greater focus on the things that are of greater value in life, and I can leave the lesser things go a lot easier. I have felt the *crush* of the Lord, and I have experienced His sustaining grace.

When Paul said that a messenger of Satan was sent to harass him, the word *harass* or *buffet* is the same word used in Matthew 26:67 to describe when Jesus was on trial and punched by the soldiers. Its root meaning is *knuckles*, and it had to do with the blows of the fist that crush the tissue and the bone. Essentially Paul said,

"I've got this thorn in my flesh that drives its knuckles into my body. It is a messenger from Satan." Could God have prevented this trial in Paul's life? Absolutely! However, God allowed it so that he would not be proud. In verse 8, Paul wrote, "Three times I pleaded with the Lord about this, that it should leave me." Have you ever gotten a good answer to why God didn't answer Paul's prayer in the way that he prayed? I mean, he was a man of prayer. He was given healing power by the Spirit for others. Why couldn't he elicit healing for himself? Some people have suggested that he didn't have enough faith. But that idea is absolutely foreign to the text and contrary to the character of Paul. Others have suggested that he didn't claim his deliverance. I don't buy that either because the text says exactly what the Lord said. Paul asked the Lord to take it away, and the Lord responded, "My grace is sufficient for you, for my power is made perfect in weakness" (verse 9). That is why Paul concluded that he should simply boast about his infirmities so that the power of Christ might rest on him.

So God gave Job over to disaster so that he would be living proof of the character of a godly man and so that he could know God in a fuller way. And God turned Christ over to Satan to prove His purity. Further, God turned Paul over to Satan so that he would remain humble and be a more effective servant.

Now let's see how God turned the apostle Peter over to Satan. In Luke 22:31 Jesus was speaking to Peter when He said, "Simon, Simon, behold, Satan demanded to have you, that he might sift you like wheat." Notice that Jesus called Peter by his original name, Simon. His name Peter means "rock," but Jesus used the name Simon because He was emphasizing the oldness He saw in Peter's behavior. In fact, Jesus said it twice because of His compassion. "Simon, Simon, Satan wants to sift you."

I believe what Satan wanted to do to Peter is what he wants to do to every follower of Christ. The Bible says that Satan goes around like a roaring lion, and his purpose is to devour every believer. You see, if Satan can capture true followers of Christ and get them to abandon their salvation (which cannot happen to a true believer, but that shows you how twisted the mind of Satan is), or in the very least swallow them up in his own evil kingdom, then in a sense he could win a victory over God. Again, as I wrote in a previous chapter, I do not believe that a true follower of Christ can or will ever lose his or her salvation, yet they can certainly give in to the schemes of the evil one and allow him to destroy their lives. Although I will never know the specifics of what happened, in some twisted way I believe Nathan gave in to the lies and the pressure of the devil, which ultimately took his life. Satan could never have Nathan's soul, but he certainly was able to destroy his physical life—a young man who had so much potential for influencing people's lives for the kingdom of God—and Satan knew it and zeroed in on him.

In the same way, Satan wanted to devour Peter because he was so crucial to the development of the church in the founding years. Satan wanted to sift him like wheat. The devil wanted to blow him away. He wanted to disintegrate him as wheat does when it is thrown into the air and it blows away the chaff. Satan wants to do the same thing to people's lives today. He wants to blow away our confidence. He wants to blow away our usefulness. He wants to blow away our trust in God and our effectiveness for God.

Do you think Jesus could have prevented it from happening? Of course He could have. The same Lord who will bind Satan for a thousand years, and eventually forever, could have bound him from touching Peter, but He didn't. Instead, Jesus prayed in verse 32, "But I have prayed for you that your faith may not fail. And when you have turned again, strengthen your brothers." What Jesus is telling Peter is that "I have prayed for you so that you won't ultimately lose your salvation." And just like God would allow Satan to go only so far with Job, He only let Satan go so far with Peter. Jesus concluded by saying, "And when you have turned again, strengthen your brothers." In other words, Jesus would let Peter go and be delivered over to Satan. We wonder why He would do that. The reason is that God was letting Peter go through this trial so that he could strengthen others. Jesus was teaching Peter humility and dependence, and He wanted someone who could tell others what it is like to be in the clutches of Satan. Jesus tells Peter, "When you have come through this trial, I want you to come back and strengthen others."

That is the same thing God wants from all of us. He will sometimes allow us to go through a trial, a buffeting from Satan, for the purpose of us being able to use our experience to encourage someone else. I am sad that our son gave in to his buffeting and lost the earthly battle, and there are so many others just like him who are also giving in to the devil and being defeated by him. It doesn't have to be that way. That is the reason I am writing these chapters. I do not want anyone else's child or any other follower of Christ to ever believe they cannot win this battle. Jesus wants us to survive, but we must make the conscious decision to turn to Him and not believe the lies we are being told by the evil one. Paul learned this lesson, and so did Peter, and they became stronger because of it. In fact, it was Peter who warned us in 1 Peter 5:8, "Be sober-minded; be watchful. Your adversary the devil prowls around like a roaring lion, seeking someone to devour." Peter knew this from his own life experience, and he took his own advice.

Let me wrap this chapter up and bring it to a concluding point. As we have been discovering, the Scriptures indicated that there are times when people who are believers in Jesus Christ, who, for God's own purposes, can be brought under the dominion of Satan, unprotected. Whether it be Hymenaeus and Alexander, who were pastors in a first-century church, or whether it is an Old Testament character like Job, or a New Testament character like Paul or Peter or even Jesus—they were all people who belonged to God's kingdom but who God delivered over to Satan for a specific purpose. Some are turned over for refining, like Peter. Some are turned over for greater effectiveness, like Paul. Some are turned over to prove the validity of their faith, like Job. However, in all of them, the greater glory goes to God, in praising Him for the kind of salvation that holds on to a Job and the kind of power that humbles a Paul and that restores a Peter. God gets the glory in it all. There is a purpose for our lives in it all.

Right now if you feel like you are going through a testing and you are wondering why it is happening, you don't have a good explanation for it, and you have been praying and seeking God and it seems like things are not getting any better, perhaps it is because God is refining you. Maybe it is because God is preparing you for greater effectiveness. Or it could be that God is simply proving your love for Him. Whatever it is, you can trust that God has a greater purpose than what you might be able to understand right now. Keep trusting Him and give Him the glory for what He is doing. Learn the lesson, and above all, never give in to the lies and schemes of the devil. One loss is too many in the soldiers of God's army. In the next chapter I'll show you some principles for dealing with strongholds in your life and how you can find freedom from them.

# Tearing Down Strongholds

Beside our house, there is a little plot of ground, about fourteen feet long and three feet wide, that I have turned into a vegetable garden. I never get a huge amount of produce out of my garden, but I plant seed in it just to see something grow. The first year I planted my little garden I noticed there had been some kind of critters getting in and chewing on things. So I went to our local farm store and purchased some chicken wire and stakes and installed a little fence around my garden. For the most part, the fence kept the big critters out. However, the next year I discovered I had chipmunks who had made their home under the air conditioner unit next to my garden and that they were eating the seed right out of the earth before they got a chance to grow. I replanted seed three times before I came up with a more permanent solution. The point is that in order to protect my garden I had to take some proactive steps in building strongholds that would keep the critters at bay.

All of us have *critters* that sneak into our lives at times. It is these critters, the enemy of our soul, that we have been talking about in the last couple of chapters. They put us in danger of losing our joy, of stealing our happiness, and of leading us down the path of misery. If we yield to them, they destroy our lives altogether, in the same way the critters would have destroyed my little garden had I not taken action to keep them away.

In this chapter, I want to show you how to pull down the strongholds that Satan wants to build in our lives and also how to build strongholds that will keep Satan at bay.

Romans 13:12 tells us, "The night is far gone; the day is at hand. So then let us cast off the works of darkness and put on the armor of light." The "day" is talking about the second coming of the Lord. The admonition is that we need to be careful to be ready in every way for when Christ returns. Part of our getting ready is to tear down strongholds we have allowed Satan to build up in our lives. I am convinced that far too many Christians have allowed Satan to harass them, oppress them, and bring bondages into their lives that keep them from experiencing freedom in Christ. Furthermore, the fearful thing is that many believers have not even considered that maybe the stronghold in their life was put there by Satan. In this chapter, I want to encourage you that you do not have to allow strongholds to control you, but you can allow God to be your rock and your fortress.

Perhaps you remember the story in 2 Samuel 22 when David was finally delivered from the hand of his enemies. He wrote in verses 1 to 2, "And David spoke to the Lord the words of this song on the day when the Lord delivered him from the hand of all his enemies, and from the hand of Saul. He said, 'The Lord is my rock and my fortress and my deliverer.'" You see, David depended on God to be his stronghold against his enemies.

After Nathan took his life, in the days following it was difficult not to try to cast blame. It seems like mankind always needs to find a scapegoat for our pain. It was tempting to blame Nathan for making poor choices that led him to the point where his fight-and-flight trigger was somehow numbed. It was tempting to blame myself for not being more intuitive, more connected, more in tune with my son's pain. I could have blamed his friends for not seeing that something was wrong and for not running to his rescue. And yet when we fall into the blame-game trap for our pain, what we are really doing is seeing ourselves or others as inept, foolish, or irresponsible. But the reality is that the more we play the blame game, the more we lose. It becomes a stronghold for Satan to get a foothold in our lives. Instead of blaming, eventually I chose to turn to the Lord as my rock and defence. I still don't have a lot of answers to the questions surrounding Nathan's actions, in the same way that David knew he was called to be the king of Israel and had no idea why God was allowing his persecution, in the same way that Job didn't understand his demise in light of his righteous lifestyle, or that Paul could possibly comprehend the full reason for his thorn in the flesh. In each case these men turned to God as their stronghold and rejected the advances of the enemy. I chose not to blame but to turn to God to uphold me.

The apostle Paul's testimony and theme of his life can be found in 2 Corinthians 10:4–6, "For the weapons of our warfare are not of the flesh but have divine power to destroy strongholds. We destroy arguments and every lofty opinion raised against the knowledge of God, and take every thought captive to obey Christ, being ready to punish every disobedience, when your obedience is complete." To destroy strongholds means to demolish and remove anything that keeps us from knowing God's presence and will in our lives. It is a crippling thing to allow these strongholds to remain in our lives. They bog us down, we stop growing spiritually, and we lose our joy.

Let me show you what some of these strongholds are. In the Old Testament, a stronghold was a fortified dwelling used as a means of protection from the enemy. For example, King David hid from King Saul in strongholds in the wilderness. First Samuel 23:14 says, "And David remained in the strongholds in the wilderness, in the hill country of the wilderness of Ziph. And Saul sought him every day, but God did not give him into his hand." Verse 19 continues, "Then the Ziphites went up to Saul at Gibeah, saying, 'Is not David hiding among us in the strongholds at Horesh, on the hill of Hachilah, which is south of Jeshimon?'" These strongholds were physical structures that were usually caves high up on a mountainside and were difficult to assault.

The Bible writers had this Old Testament imagery in mind when they adapted the word *stronghold* to define powerful, vigorously protected spiritual realities. Therefore, a stronghold is a source of protection for us from the devil. The Lord becomes our stronghold. A stronghold is a source of defense from the devil's influence in our lives. This is what Paul is talking about in Romans 6:16 when he said, "Do you not know that if you present yourselves to anyone as obedient slaves, you are slaves of the one whom you obey, either of sin, which leads to death, or of obedience, which leads to righteousness?" In other words, when we become sympathetic to the evil influences and thoughts that the devil puts in our minds, we become a slave to those influences which will determine the direction of our lives. However, when we run to the Lord, He becomes a stronghold and a defense for our minds and hearts.

Let's look at the New Testament definition of a stronghold as Paul defines it. He defines a stronghold as speculations or lofty things raised up against the knowledge of God. Paul says it this way in 2 Corinthians 10:5, "We destroy arguments and every lofty opinion raised against the knowledge of God, and take every thought captive to obey Christ." The word *arguments* is another word for *strongholds*. It is any kind of thinking that exalts itself above the knowledge of God. You see, there are walls of resistance that can build up in our minds, and they need to be torn down. These strongholds are any reasonings that are opposed to the truth of God's Word. It is the pride of intelligence that exalts itself. Paul is not attacking intelligence, but he is attacking intellectualism. It is that high-minded attitude that makes people think they know more than they really do. As a result, it gives the devil a place of influence in a person's thought life, and it needs to be torn down. Paul declared in Romans 6:6, "We know that our old self was crucified with him in order that the body of sin might be brought to nothing, so that we would no longer be enslaved to sin." When Christ came into our lives as Lord and Savior, He took off the shackles of sin and set us free from the bondage of sin's power. When we're talking about strongholds, we're not just talking about random thoughts or occasional sins, but we are talking about areas in our life where we are in bondage and we are having a hard time breaking loose.

There are a number of ways that strongholds take root in our life. First, they can come from worldly influence. In previous chapters, we looked at the meaning of 1 John 5:19, "The whole world lies in the power of the evil one." Since we live in a world that is under the influence of Satan, it makes sense that many strongholds are the result of an accumulation of uncrucified thoughts and unsanctified attitudes that have ruled in our lives. As children growing up under the sway of the wicked one, there is a steady stream of information and experiences that continually shape our childhood perceptions. That's why it is so important to protect the minds of our children. The sense of identity in a child is shaped by any number of influences. It is shaped by the love or the lack of love found in a home. Identity is influenced by cultural norms and environments, by peer values and pressures, as well as by fear of rejection, physical appearance, and intelligence and what they learn at home or in the classroom. That is why Paul says in Romans 12:2, "Do not be conformed to this world, but be transformed by the renewal of your mind." We must allow God's thoughts from His Word to transform, renew, and cleanse our minds from unrighteousness and the world's influences.

\*\*\*\*\*

## Barbara

Are you familiar with the phrase "Keep a short list?" I heard it probably decades ago. At the time I believed it referred to our relationships with other people. In other words, don't keep track of wrongs, but take care of them as quick as you can. Some time after, I came upon the verse in Psalm 139:23–24, "Search me, O God, and know my heart! Try me and know my thoughts! And see if there be any grievous way in me, and lead me in the way everlasting." At the time, I had been encouraged by an older woman to not only begin the day with my quiet time as I had been doing, but to end my day with these verses as a model for prayer. In other words, keep a short list. Over the years as I head to bed, I have found it much easier to look back over my day and question if there was an action, words, or thoughts and ask the Lord to reveal to me if I had gone astray or anything I needed to confess. I have found this liberating, freeing me from allowing any potential of a stronghold to get a grip in my life. Too often in the busyness of life, we fall into bed, have a rest, and wake up the next day ready to proceed with whatever that day holds. Too often if we are carrying any anxious thought or action that may be offensive to the Lord, and it becomes easy and habitual to have one thing pile on top of the other. And then we end up with a stronghold. I have also found that as I practice this quietness, at the end of the day, I start to sense God's leading earlier in the day and to pass anything to Him that might be a burden to me.

\*\*\*\*\*

For those of us who are followers of Christ, we scratch our heads, wondering how some intelligent people can think the way they do about certain things in life. I am sure you can fill in the blanks of many things we are concerned about. But then we realize that people have twisted thoughts because they do not have any other way to think. They have worldly minds that are influenced by the wicked one, and they will protect and defend their ideas, and they will justify their opinions as though they were born out of their own creativity. They do not even know Satan has influenced them. As a result, the essence of who we are is an accumulation of our thought life and who or what influences it. Proverbs 23:7 warns us, "For as he thinks in his hearts, so is he" (NKJV). That means that if our parents or schoolteachers or grandparents shape our thoughts and opinions, it does not matter how good those people are. If their opinions are not of God, then they are wrong opinions. I am not saying that everything they said was wrong and was a bad influence. I will not have you blaming your parents for every bad choice you have made in your life. However, I am saying that those things that deal with morality, right and wrong, the choices of life, right thinking, and eternal things must find as its basis of truth what God says in His Word. Isaiah 55:7–9 says, "Let the wicked forsake his way, and the unrighteous man his thoughts; let him return to the Lord, that he may have compassion on him, and to our God, for he will abundantly pardon. 'For my thoughts are not your thoughts, neither are your ways my ways,' declares the Lord. 'For as the heavens are higher than the earth, so are my ways higher than your ways and my thoughts than your thoughts.'" There are some people who will call Christians narrow-minded or that we cannot think for ourselves. However, the problem with that accusation is that none of us really think for ourselves. People and things influence all of us, but we are also influenced by either God or the wicked one. As Christians, we admit that God influences our thinking. On the other hand, the world and those without Christ will not admit that the wicked one influences their thinking and through those he controls. So, in reality, as a follower of God I am no more narrow-minded than anyone else. It is all dependent on whom we chose to follow.

Now before I get into some solutions for dealing with strong-holds, I feel I need to talk about some common strongholds people deal with. Simply because we are Christians, it does not mean we are exempt from having to wrestle with strongholds in our lives. Even Christians struggle with fear, resentment, bitterness, unforgiveness, apathy, unbelief, depression, anxiety, being lukewarm, sinful thoughts, lust, pride, greed, drug abuse, various addictions, just to name a few.

Here is the difficulty with dealing with those strongholds. We may justify our strongholds by saying things like "I'm this way because so and so makes me this way," "You didn't grow up in my home," "I'm no worse than anyone else." "It's not a big deal. Everyone is doing it." "I like the way I am and I could not change even if I wanted to. It's just the way I am." Or even "I'll never get over it, so I just better get used to it." These excuses remind me of Proverbs 23:7, which I quoted earlier, "For as he thinks in his heart, so is he." That means that before any deliverance can be accomplished, we have to honestly recognize and confess our need. Examine your heart and see if there is any area in your life that feels hopeless. That's a stronghold. Any area where you feel like you are resisting change, any area where you feel like you can never conquer, anything that feels like it has a strong grip on you and that nothing could ever help, are all strong-holds that must be torn down.

Let me give you some faith principles from the Bible for pulling down strongholds. You have probably already discovered that you cannot tear them down in your own power or by your own wit. We must use scriptural principles to tear down spiritual strongholds.

Paul said in 2 Corinthians 10:4–5, "For the weapons of our warfare are not of the flesh but have divine power to destroy strongholds. We destroy arguments and every lofty opinion raised against the knowledge of God, and take every thought captive to obey Christ." I see two principles in these verses that will help us to tear down strongholds in our life. First is to bring our thoughts into captivity to Christ. A literal translation of verse 5 says, "We take every thought captive and make it obey Christ." In other words, if all the arguments on any subject are brought to us by the world's way of thinking, run those thoughts through the filter of God's Word and get your thoughts corrected as to what God has to say. Not every thought that comes from the world is incorrect, but the filter of God's Word will quickly bring it to light if it is.

I was in a store recently, making a purchase. I gave the cashier a $20 bill. She took it and ran a marker over it and then exposed it to an ultraviolet light. If the bill had have been counterfeit, the ultraviolet light would have shown the truth. That is what the Word of God does with the thoughts of this world. All those wrong thoughts that lead us to disobey Christ must be captured and crucified, and then we must allow God's thoughts to capture us and permeate us until they become part of us. You see, the only one who has the right to shape our lives is Jesus Christ. Paul said in Romans 3:4, "Let God be true though every one were a liar, as it is written, 'That you may be justified in your words, and prevail when you are judged.'" We must determine not to allow anyone nor anything other than Christ to shape us unless they are consistent with the Word of God. Every thought that enters our mind is a possible devise that Satan can use to set us against God. Every argument, every thought, is a scheme or a concoction that is directed against the true knowledge of God. It is an act of the will that we bring all our intellectual activity into complete subjection to Christ.

Principle number two is that our obedience brings us into the stronghold of Christ's likeness. The goal of breaking strongholds involves more than simply getting our burdens or even Satan off our back. The real goal is that God is working to move us into conformity with the image of Christ. This is how Paul put it in Romans

8:28–29, "And we know that for those who love God all things work together for good, for those who are called according to his purpose. For those whom he foreknew he also predestined to be conformed to the image of his Son, in order that he might be the first-born among many brothers." In other words, the way to realize God's ultimate victory is to reach toward God's ultimate goal, which is to be transformed into the likeness of Christ. What so many people fail to understand is that it is not us as followers of Christ that the devil is afraid of, but he is afraid of Christ in us. Therefore, victory over Satan begins with the name of Jesus on our lips, and it is consummated by the nature of Jesus in our heart. James 4:7 says, "Submit yourselves therefore to God. Resist the devil, and he will flee from you." Simply speaking, whatever it is that we are struggling with—a fear, depression, a sinful thought, negative words spoken to us by someone that we are believing—submit all those thoughts to God, repent of your unbelief, and yield yourself to God. It is better to develop holiness in our lives than it is spending our time praying against the devil because it is the joy of the Lord that defeats depression, it is living a life of faith that destroys unbelief, and it is aggressive love that casts out fear. As we continually yield ourselves to Christ by surrendering ourselves to Him, we literally build an impenetrable stronghold of God's presence around us.

Maybe you are going through a season of conflict and turmoil right now. It is a good thing if you recognize it because it shows your desire to be free. Now is the time to begin exercising your authority in Christ by resisting the devil. It begins with the name of Jesus on your lips, and it continues by allowing the nature of Christ to form in your heart. First Peter 5:8–9 says, "Be sober-minded; be watchful. Your adversary the devil prowls around like a roaring lion, seeking someone to devour. Resist him, firm in your faith, knowing that the same kinds of suffering are being experienced by your brotherhood throughout the world." Notice those words *firm in your faith*. That is the yielding part of what you need to do. As you stand firm in your faith, it will remove Satan's ability to influence your mind. That is when you will see that the weapons of your warfare are mighty for the pulling down of strongholds.

Perhaps as we close this chapter you would like to say a prayer, something like this: "Lord, you know what I'm struggling with today. [Take a minute to identify your struggle.] Today I am declaring victory over this stronghold in my life because I am yielding myself to you and I am allowing you to develop your nature in me. Transform my mind and make me into your likeness. I realize that I will be in process, but teach me your ways." You may have to pray a prayer like that many times, but keep praying, and keep yielding, and keep trusting, and you will begin to see and feel a difference as Christ forms His likeness in you.

# Joy Down in My Heart

## 1 Thessalonians 5:16

One of the disciplines of the Christian life that has puzzled and even eluded many people over the years is the discipline of *joy*. We tend to confuse joy with happiness. We think that if we are happy, we will have joy. Or if we have joy, it must mean we are happy.

One reason for writing this chapter is because I fear that Nathan may have been confused about this subject. He wrote in a note he left behind that he never had joy in his life and that it was something he was seeking. Yet we look back at pictures of him when he was young, and he was always smiling, he was an easy-to-get-along-with child, and although quiet, he was very likeable and other children liked being with him. It is puzzling as to why Nathan may have felt as if he never knew joy, which brings me to the conclusion that he didn't really understand true biblical joy, not unlike so many other people. In this chapter I have set about the task to solve the puzzle of a lack of joy so many say they feel.

The book of Psalms references joy more than any other book in the Bible. The Psalms references joy in passages like Psalm 16:11, "You make known to me the path of life; in your presence there is fullness of joy." Psalm 95:1 says, "Oh come, let us sing to the Lord; let us make a joyful noise to the rock of our salvation!" Psalm 149:5 says, "Let the godly exult in glory; let them sing for joy on their beds." The apostle Peter wrote in 1 Peter 1:8, "Though you have not seen him, you love him. Though you do not now see him, you believe in him and rejoice with joy that is inexpressible and filled with glory." James wrote in James 1:2, "Count it all joy, my brothers, when you meet trials of various kinds." The author of Hebrews says that it is actually joy that enabled Jesus to endure the cross when he wrote in Hebrews 12:2, "Looking to Jesus, the founder and perfecter of our faith, who for the joy that was set before him endured the cross, despising the shame, and is seated at the right hand of the throne of God." Those are all great verses and, in some ways, comforting verses. However, what is the *joy* they are all talking about? What does it mean to have biblical joy, and how do we get it?

To answer those questions, let's begin by looking at 1 Thessalonians 5:16. There are a number of verses we could go to in our study that speaks of joy, but I want us to begin with this passage because it is so concise, so inescapable, and so direct. This verse simply says, "Rejoice always." That's it! In fact, in the original language the adverb comes first and it reads, "Always rejoice." The command is in the present tense so that the later part would read, "Always continue to rejoice—always be rejoicing." It is this command and the attitude of joy that I want to talk about in this chapter.

There is plenty of reason in our world to feel sad, upset, stressed, and full of fear and doubt, but not for the Christian. We are commanded to rejoice always. By the way, this is not an isolated command. In the book of Philippians, Paul talks about joy no less than seventeen times. One of the most famous verses in Philippians is found in chapter 4, verse 4, where Paul said, "Rejoice in the Lord always; again I will say, rejoice." We are commanded to rejoice and to have joy. Pastor John MacArthur says, "There is no event and there are no circumstances in life that should diminish the Christian's joy." Now that's a pretty bold and hard-hitting statement. However, the reality is that the Bible commands us to rejoice. How often? Always!

Let's begin by looking at the command: "Rejoice always." As I already said, this is not an isolated command. I think of 1 Peter 4:13 that says, "But rejoice insofar as you share Christ's sufferings, that you may also rejoice and be glad when his glory is revealed." In other words, he is saying that the more we suffer, the more we need to rejoice. For example, I think of Jesus's discourse in the upper room the night before He was arrested. In John 13, we read about the last supper Jesus had with His disciples, and from there, right around the corner to John 17, we find an amazing dialogue in which Jesus leaves a legacy to them and to us. One of the gems Jesus leaves is His own joy. Eight times in John 17 Jesus refers to joy or to full joy. In paraphrasing what Jesus said, He says to them, "I'm leaving, I'm going to die, I'm going to be crucified, I'm not going to be here, I'm not going to be with you. You're going to have trouble. Those leading the synagogue will come after you and take your life, etc." But then He says, "I tell you all these things because I want you to have joy." Wow! Really? In the face of all those circumstances, He wants them and us to be full of joy? Yes. Jesus continually stressed this point, and circumstances never change it.

Look at what Jesus taught in Matthew 5:10–12a, "Blessed are those who are persecuted for righteousness' sake, for theirs is the kingdom of heaven. Blessed are you when others revile you and persecute you and utter all kinds of evil against you falsely on my account. Rejoice and be glad." I would be lying if I said that being glad when you have been insulted, and persecuted, and all kinds of evil things have been said against you falsely is easy. There is a similar passage found in Luke 6:22–23, "Blessed are you when people hate you and when they exclude you and revile you and spurn your name as evil, on account of the Son of Man! Rejoice in that day, and leap for joy, for behold, your reward is great in heaven; for so their fathers did to the prophets." The word *blessed* means to be happy. It would be like if you arrive home after a hard day at work and you are whistling a tune and singing a song and a smile is across your face from ear to ear. Maybe you are even doing a little jig, and your spouse asks, "What happened to you?" And you respond, "Oh, I was persecuted today, and insulted, and ostracized by people in the office, and all kinds of people were saying untrue things about me, I really got worked over today." I'm sure your spouse would respond, "Are you sure you're all right?" Well, the truth is you might not be singing and dancing, but what we ought to be asking ourselves in those circumstances that come into our lives is "What is God trying to accomplish in me through this experience?" The bottom line is that God is trying to make us more like His Son.

But then we ask, "What about the *leaping for joy* part?" Does that seem like something we should be doing? If we obey the command to rejoice, how often should we rejoice? The answer is that we are to rejoice always, even when we are not being persecuted or going through some hard trial and when we are being persecuted or going through some hard trial. We're to rejoice always. How can we do that? The apostle Paul seemed pretty good at rejoicing always. But then he had to be because his whole life was one of pain. James is instructive on this point when he said in James 1:2, "Count it all joy, my brothers, when you meet trials of various kinds." In other words, we ought to be more joyful when we find ourselves in a trial than when we are experiencing the good times because trials are so much more refining and they are so much more spiritually productive. Trials tend to convince us that we are not in control of everything or maybe of anything. They strip us of our pride and make us more dependent on God. They enhance our prayer life. James goes on to say in verses 3 to 4, "For you know that the testing of your faith produces steadfastness. And let steadfastness have its full effect, that you may be perfect and complete, lacking in nothing." Let me ask you a pointed, soul-searching question. Do you rejoice in your trials and pain as much as complain about them? To be honest, I find myself complaining more than I care to be, but instead, we are called to rejoice in our pain and trials. Not because of them, but in them. Take care to notice the difference.

Now you might be thinking, "Romans 12:15 says, 'Rejoice with those who rejoice, weep with those who weep.' Isn't that a contradiction?" That's a good question. Is there ever a time to stop rejoicing? Yes, in an outward sense. Like when a friend comes to you feeling overwhelmed by something or a problem they are going through. Maybe they start crying, and you feel sympathy or empathy for them, and perhaps you feel comfortable enough to put your arm around them and even cry with them. However, your friend's pain should not affect your joy, and neither should it affect their joy. You see, underneath the pain and the tears is unending joy, at all times. By the way, this thinking was such a part of the early church that when they greeted one another they would say "Chairo," which means "Rejoice." In our culture we say hi or "How's it going?" But in the New Testament church they would greet one another and say, "Rejoice." They reminded each other of the command to rejoice whenever they greeted one another.

Remember how, after the resurrection of Christ, He met the women coming from the empty tomb, and in Matthew 28:9 He greeted them by saying, "Rejoice." Again, in Acts 15 a letter was sent to the council of Jerusalem, and it said in verse 23, "With the following letter: 'The brothers, both the apostles and the elders, to the brothers who are of the Gentiles in Antioch and Syria and Cilicia, greetings.'" The Greek word that has been translated "greetings" is really "rejoice."

Furthermore, when we are talking about joy in a biblical sense, it is different from the joy the world experiences. The joy of the world is completely connected with earthly pleasure. The world rushes toward their impulses and they fulfill their every want, but it is short-lived. That's why Proverbs 14:13 says, "Even in laughter the heart may ache, and the end of joy may be grief." You see, the world's kind of joy is fleeting and doesn't last beyond the pleasure itself. So I'm not talking about some kind of pleasure fulfillment. Joy is not having some sort of personality trait. You've heard it said before, "Oh, she's so happy all the time." No, that's not it. It's not a positive thinking approach that says, "Just be happy." And I'm not talking about playing mental games. In fact, what I am talking about isn't even a natural thing for us to do or to be. I am talking about a supernatural joy that only belongs to Christians. It is something that is deep down inside. The source of our joy is identified in Galatians 5:22 as a fruit of the Spirit. In fact, Romans 14:17 says, "For the kingdom of God is not a matter of eating and drinking but of righteousness and peace and joy in the Holy Spirit." I'm talking about a spiritual joy that comes from the Holy Spirit, the same as spiritual peace and righteousness and love. It is a joy that comes from God through Christ and is dispensed by the Holy Spirit, a joy that no circumstance can ever steal away. Why? Because this kind of joy isn't just a feeling of silly happiness that bursts out in laughter, but it is a joy that says, "Things are okay because I am putting my trust in God." It is the confidence of knowing that whatever happens to us, things are going to be all right because God is in control and He is being glorified. That is why in everything we can give thanks with joy because it causes us to wonder what God is doing in our lives and that He is in control, whatever it is.

Now that we know what true biblical joy is, let's look at some reasons why we need to obey this command to rejoice. First, joy is a response to the character of God. In other words, joy begins when we look back and we know that our sovereign and loving Father has our well-being in mind and that He is working it all out for our good. We cannot always rejoice in our circumstances, but we can rejoice in the character of God. I'm not just saying the words, but this is something I have had to live out as we have been on this journey of grief. I do not rejoice that our Son is no longer with us here on earth, but I must continually remind myself that God's character is always good and that He is always working for my good. You see, God is unchanging in character and always consistent. What if God wasn't that way? What if God changed the way He operated from time to time? That's a scary thought, isn't it? What if His grace was whimsical, and He only dispensed it on certain occasions when He felt like it? What if His justice came and went? What if He had mental lapses? What if He was good most of the time, or seven out of ten times? That's not the God we know, and it is not His character. The character of God is absolute and unchanging, and that is a cause for joy.

Also, joy is a proper act of appreciation for the work of Christ. When we realize that Jesus bore the cost for our sins and that Jesus knew no sin but became sin for us, that we were redeemed with the blood of Christ and that even though we were His enemy He died for us anyway, and that Christ has accomplished for us, it gives us an abiding joy that no circumstance on earth can affect.

Thirdly, we ought to have joy as an act of confidence in the work of the Holy Spirit. When you stop to think about it, what is the work of the Holy Spirit? Well, remember I already said previously that part of the fruit of the Spirit is joy. In addition, remember that

Romans 14:17 says that He brings joy, among other things. Also remember that 2 Corinthians 3:18 says that the Spirit moves us along from glory to glory in our likeness of Jesus. Not only that, but the Spirit lives in us and shows us Christ. He leads us into all truth. He brings all things to our remembrance. He teaches us all things about God. He is our down payment for an eternal inheritance. He protects us from sin. The Holy Spirit seals us until the day of redemption, and He fills our mouths with praise. Those are all really great reasons to rejoice.

We also rejoice as a response to all the blessings we have been given. For example, Ephesians 1:3 says, "Blessed be the God and Father of our Lord Jesus Christ, who has blessed us in Christ with every spiritual blessing in the heavenly places." Now someone might be thinking, "My life doesn't really feel like it has been blessed right now." In response I would remind you that every time you sin, when you confess it, that sin is forgiven instantly. Furthermore, every time God moves you one more step toward the image of Christ, that's monumental. And every time God refines you through a trial, that's a blessing. Every time God gives a provision, every time He brings you through another day, every time He gives you the power not to yield to temptation, every time He guards you from things that could happen that you don't even know about, it gives us reason to feel blessed. Plus, the Spirit is always interceding for us, calling on God to bring us blessing and joy each day. The Spirit does all this and more in order to bring us blessings every day. How can we not say we are blessed?

Joy is also our response to the providence of God. God's providence is the reality that God orchestrates all the circumstances that create something good for us. Now if I were God and could do anything I want, in my humanness I'd probably just go out and make things happen. If I wanted something done, I wouldn't wait for humans to do it for me, but I'd do it myself. That's just my personality. Maybe some of you are like that. But I'm thankful that God isn't like me and that He waits for all the billions of contingencies to happen, and then somehow He puts it all together for our good and makes something beautiful. That's what Romans 8:28 is all about.

You see, God isn't in heaven wringing His hands saying, "Whew, I didn't know that would happen! How am I going to fix that?" Our confidence is in knowing that God is in control of everything and that He uses everything for our good.

Joy is a response to the promise of our future glory. Paul said in Colossians 3:2, "Set your minds on things that are above, not on things that are on earth." Paul wasn't saying something that might be painful to the Colossian believers, like "You need to clean out your mind even though it hurts." Rather, he was telling them something that would free them from all the crippling preoccupations of this earth that doesn't matter anyway. Our joy is precipitated, not by what is today, but what will be tomorrow.

If we don't have joy in our lives, there might be a few reasons for this. Maybe the reason is because you don't know Christ as your Savior and Lord. The first step for you is to agree with God that you are a sinner and then accept His free gift of forgiveness. Acknowledge Him as your Savior and Lord and allow Him the control of your life. Or perhaps joy is absent from your life because there is something that is going on in your life where you are allowing Satan to steal your joy away. First Peter 5:8 says, "Be sober-minded; be watchful. Your adversary the devil prowls around like a roaring lion, seeking someone to devour." Peter then gives the solution when he says in verse 7, "Casting all your anxieties on him because he cares for you."

Whatever it is that is taking away your joy, throw it onto Christ and allow Him to carry the burden and restore your joy. But then maybe you don't have joy because you have false expectations that are connected to pride. It is the sin of saying to yourself, "I don't have enough. I want more of that. I deserve having that." The premise of advertising is to make us feel dissatisfied with what we have, and ingratitude will always be a joy-killer. Finally, not having sound doctrine can take your joy away. With everything that goes on in our lives, if all we ever do is live by our feelings we are gong to be a mess all the time. It would be like a pilot of an airplane trying to fly the plane without a manual or without a backup plan if something goes wrong. In that case, they would be flying on emotions, and it could turn into flight 857 to heaven. However, having sound doctrine helps to keep your life steady and in control. Sound doctrine points us to the truth that God is in control.

You see, if our mind is controlled by the Word of God, that's how our emotions are going to respond. So rejoice always. That's the response of a person who puts their trust in God and says, "God has got this. He is in control, and I am at perfect peace." Sometimes that realization is reflected in an emotional response, but mostly, it is the ability to stay calm, feel at peace, and stay on our feet through the storm. Let's choose joy and let God be God.

*****

*Barbara*

As I read Mark's words, my mind is racing. Where do I start to share even a bit of my journey to understanding joy? His last line, "Let's choose joy," is major. Maybe I would add to it, "Let's choose God." I think back to the time as a nine-year-old that I felt led to make a decision at the invitation for salvation. I accepted the invitation, and the Bible declared that at the moment I accepted Jesus Christ as my Savior, He cleansed me from all my sins. However, what does a nine-year-old really know about following Christ? It was in my teen years, as I grappled with ongoing issues that were going on around me, that I felt called to rededicate my life to the Lord at a worship service I was attending. In that moment, I still didn't understand it all, but I knew that God was calling me forward. A couple of years later, I would make my third significant choice during a church service when the invitation was about being called to full-time ministry. I did not know what God wanted with my life, but there was a calling to listen and obey. It will be fifty years ago this fall that I started down the path of choosing God. What has become clear to me is that I can ask God for forgiveness for my sins, but that does not necessarily mean I have allowed Him to be Lord of my life.

It has been the times in these fifty years that I have consciously chosen God that have made the path clearer. The words that we generally use to describe human experiences does not touch what

God desires for us. In our humanness we can only understand them with our finite minds. The excitement on Christmas morning or at a birthday celebration or when seeing family who we haven't seen for a while becomes our joy. All of those experiences are wonderful and full of smiles and happiness, but after experiencing the loss of Nathan, my definition of joy has expanded beyond any experience I have ever known.

Anyone who saw me the first several months or even longer after Nathan died would never suggest that I had joy. That is because I was mourning. I was in deep grief from the shock of his unexpected death at a time when we were looking forward to his wedding and a time of rich celebration. However, it was in that time of mourning and grieving that God was with me, carrying me along, healing me and wiping my tears, and showing me more of His love than I ever knew.

It is possible to have joy in the midst of crushing loss because my joy is not in experiencing happiness or the great excitement of popular circumstances that create excitement. It is by choosing God as often as I have needed to choose God and by choosing to accept and obey the truth of His word in my life that God has taught me that my joy and my peace is from Him and is in the depths of me. No one, no pain, can erase His presence in my life

# How to Have Joy in Every Situation
## Philippians 1:12–26

In the previous chapter, I talked about how joy is actually a command in the Scriptures. I pointed you to 1 Thessalonians 5:16 that tells us to "rejoice always." I spoke about how joy is a fruit of the Spirit that comes as a package deal with all the other fruits of the Spirit when we invite Christ to come into our lives. I also spoke about how joy is not some kind of silly feeling that might be associated with happiness, but rather, it is a deep-down sense in our spirit that everything is okay, and we are at peace because God is in control of everything. I hope that the last chapter on joy was helpful to you, as so many people are not experiencing the joy of the Lord.

In this chapter, I want to go one step further and talk about how to have joy in every situation. Some people don't really enjoy life as much as they endure it. For them, life becomes a series of chores and obstacles that they have to go through and just endure. The dream of "if only" fills their minds constantly: "If only I could find the right job"; "If only I could retire"; "If only I could buy this, that, or the other thing." But here's a question we should be asking ourselves: Is it possible for us to have joy even if we do not have the "if-onlys?"

To come to terms with the above question, let me remind you that joy is not at all contingent on being in the right circumstances or having the right stuff. Those things might be related to happiness, but happiness is short-lived and fleeting. Real joy is internal and can never be taken away from us, regardless of the circumstances in our lives. Real joy comes to us as a gift from the Holy Spirit as one of the fruits of the Spirit. It is not so much of an emotional experience as it is recognizing that God is in control of everything, that He is working everything out for our good, and that we can be in perfect peace while in the midst of the storm.

The apostle Paul talks a lot about joy in the book of Philippians. When Paul wrote his letter to the church in Philippi, he had been in prison for the previous four years for his faith. He spent two years in a prison in Caesarea on a trumped-up charge, and then he had been put on a ship to go to Rome to appear before Nero, who was not known for his nice treatment of Christians. On the way to Rome he had been shipwrecked, stranded on an island, bitten by a poisonous snake, waited the winter on an island, continued to Rome, and spent another two years in prison waiting trial. Every four hours he got a new guard. With that as a context, read this passage in Philippians 1:12–26:

> I want you to know, brothers, that what has happened to me has really served to advance the gospel, so that it has become known throughout the whole imperial guard and to all the rest that my imprisonment is for Christ. And most of the brothers, having become confident in the Lord by my imprisonment, are much more bold to speak the word without fear. Some indeed preach Christ from envy and rivalry, but others from good will. The latter do it out of love, knowing that I am put here for the defense of the gospel. The former proclaim Christ out of selfish ambition, not sincerely but thinking to afflict me in my imprisonment. What then? Only that in every way, whether in pretense or in truth, Christ is proclaimed, and in that I rejoice. Yes, and I will rejoice, for I know that through your prayers and the help of the Spirit of Jesus

Christ this will turn out for my deliverance, as it is my eager expectation and hope that I will not be at all ashamed, but that with full courage now as always Christ will be honored in my body, whether by life or by death. For to me to live is Christ, and to die is gain. If I am to live in the flesh, that means fruitful labor for me. Yet which I shall choose I cannot tell. I am hard pressed between the two. My desire is to depart and be with Christ, for that is far better. But to remain in the flesh is more necessary on your account. Convinced of this, I know that I will remain and continue with you all, for your progress and joy in the faith, so that in me you may have ample cause to glory in Christ Jesus because of my coming to you again.

How was Paul able to show joy in the midst of all of that happening in his life? What was his secret? How did he triumph over troubles, delight in difficulties, and stay positive and joyful? In this section, I see five principles for joyful living. This is kind of the how-to for living a joyful life.

First, we must look at life from God's perspective. The fact of the matter is that we all have problems. Some of us have big problems and some have small problems, but they are all problems. Everyone carries their problems with them wherever they go—as they go to work, as they go to church, and as they do everything in life—and it affects everything. However, here is the secret we learn from Paul. The way we look at our problems is more important than the problem itself. We can look at our problems as barriers that keep us from experiencing the joy of the Lord, or we can look at them as a sort of causeway that leads us into the arms of God. Look again at what Paul wrote in verses 12b to 13, "What has happened to me has really served to advance the gospel, so that it has become known throughout the whole imperial guard and to all the rest that my imprisonment is for Christ." Paul saw his problems as an opportunity to see God do something that couldn't have been done otherwise. For him, it was so that the gospel could be preached in a place where it was never heard before. When Nathan died, both Barb and I made a commitment that if God works everything out for our good, then we need to make sure something good comes out of this tragedy. So we set out hearts and minds on listening to God and looking for opportunities to bring about something good.

One step we took, which we believe will bring about some good, was to set up a bursary in Nathan's name at Word of Life Bible Institute in Own Sound, Ontario, from where he graduated. We wanted to make sure his legacy carried on in other students who want to go on and serve the Lord. Nathan was a servant and loved the Lord. He served at summer camps for many years, worked in the youth ministry at our church, and made himself available to almost anyone who needed a hand with anything. That is the kind of legacy we don't want people to forget. Furthermore, I am writing this book as a way to help others who have gone through a tragedy in their life, in hopes that what we have gone through will benefit others and that Nathan's life prior to his death will continue to impact people. Our pain is great, as was Paul's. We continue to grieve, and yet we choose to see our problem as an opportunity for God to do something that could not have been done otherwise.

The second part of verse 12 reads like this in the *Messenger Bible*, "Instead of being squelched, the Message has actually prospered." In other words, what Satan meant for harm actually turned into something very good. You see, God is big enough to take any of our worst circumstances and turn them around for good. God can take the very worst event, like suicide, the most terrible tragedy, and flip it around and use it for something great. If God did it with the cross of Calvary, what makes us think He can't do it with our problems, no matter how large or small?

Paul was thrown into prison and bound with chains, and verses 13 to 14 say, "So that it has become known throughout the whole imperial guard and to all the rest that my imprisonment is for Christ. And most of the brothers, having become confident in the Lord by my imprisonment, are much more bold to speak the word without fear." Other Christians who were also being persecuted looked at Paul in prison and they saw his courageous attitude, and it actually encouraged them to be bolder in the faith. Courage is always contagious. Paul was taking to heart his own words found in Romans 8:28, "And we know that for those who love God all things work together for good, for those who are called according to his purpose."

If we are going to have joy in life, we must begin by getting the right perspective to our problems. We must back up from the painting of life, see the picture as a whole, and get God's perspective. When we do that, the little black mark on the painting of our life might just look like a big black splotch close-up, but when we back up and look at the painting as a whole, that black splotch is actually the part that makes the painting beautiful. To paraphrase Paul, he said, "My perspective is that whatever I am going through gives people greater access to the gospel, and that brings me joy."

Another thing that will bring joy is to get our priorities right. Not only do we need the right perspective, we also need to discover God's priority. We need to discover what is important and what is not important. If we do not find the right priorities, we end up spinning our wheels and being reactive instead of being proactive. In fact, we end up living life by simply running from one problem to the next but never really solving anything. Paul says in verses 15 to 17, "Some indeed preach Christ from envy and rivalry, but others from good will. The latter do it out of love, knowing that I am put here for the defense of the gospel. The former proclaim Christ out of selfish ambition, not sincerely but thinking to afflict me in my imprisonment." What he is saying is that it is wonderful that Christ is being preached, whether it is out of strife or envy or love. He says that he would rather that the gospel be preached out of love, but he would rejoice that it is being proclaimed at all. Some preachers might have the wrong motive, and maybe their style isn't very good or their delivery stinks, but the message is getting out there, so why does it matter?

Now someone might say, "But if the gospel isn't preached out of love, that's just wrong." But listen to what Paul said in verse 18, "What then? Only that in every way, whether in pretense or in truth,

Christ is proclaimed, and in that I rejoice. Yes, and I will rejoice." In other words, he didn't care about motives, whether mixed or bad or indifferent. However, every time one of them opens their mouth, Christ was being proclaimed, and he was happy about that. He said that he would keep on celebrating because he knew how it was going to turn out. One thing I have learned in life and in being in people work all these years is that if you want something to steal your joy quicker than anything else, then start listening to everyone who criticizes you, including you own self-criticism. Believe me when I say that regardless of what you do in life, someone is going to criticize you. If it isn't someone else, then you'll criticize yourself. It's just a part of human nature and human flesh to criticize. And if you want your joy to be stolen from you, then start listening to the critics. Let it soak in. Mull over it in your mind as often as you can. Meditate on the criticism and repeat it over and over again in your mind, and you too can be joy-free! But no one wants to be joy-free. Do you? A better solution is to do what God wants you to do and not pay attention to the critics. Set your priorities on God's priorities. Paul proclaimed that he wouldn't allow anyone to steal away his joy because joy comes by setting proper priorities, and those priorities need to be God's priorities.

A third way to have joy in every situation is to live in God's power and not your own. All of us need strength to make it through life. Quite frankly, I'm not sure how anyone does it without God. Life can wear you out and drain you completely. If I had not had the power of the Lord in these years since Nathan died, I would have been completely drained of any will to get through another day. Grief work is something that can exhaust you from the inside out. It tears at your emotions daily. It can occupy your mind relentlessly. It will distract you from living life. Without God's power it's no wonder so many people allow their losses and disappointments, and pain take them out of real living. Maybe there is someone reading this book right now who has thrown in the towel, and you need a fresh power supply.

Listen to what Paul wrote in verse 19, "For I know that through your prayers and the help of the Spirit of Jesus Christ this will turn out for my deliverance." Can you see the source of his strength? Paul gained strength through the prayers of other people. I too have found that my greatest source of strength has been through the prayers of others. During the early weeks and months after our loss, we literally felt the hands of God upon us, lifting us up day by day. If you have ever prayed for someone who has had a great loss or is suffering a great pain and you wondered if your prayers made any difference, believe me, they do. The strength given from God through your prayers are a life breath to those going through a dark valley. I can't even imagine where I would be today if it wasn't for the strength we received from God as a result of the prayers of others. It is something I could never adequately describe, but when people are praying for you, you can literally feel the strength from God coming up from underneath you and holding you up.

Paul also said that he got strength by God's supply through the Holy Spirit. Prayer is powerful, and Jesus even said we need prayer for strength when He proclaimed in Luke 21:36, "But stay awake at all times, praying that you may have strength to escape all these things that are going to take place, and to stand before the Son of Man." I believe that prayer and the power through the Holy Spirit are linked together. I don't think Paul was in prison and was able to remain strong in rejoicing because of his own willpower. However, he was strong and rejoicing because people prayed for him, and those prayers released the power of the Holy Spirit to sustain him. We need to pray for one another, and we need people to pray for us because it is through prayer, which releases the power of the Holy Spirit, that we find joy in our trials.

Psalm 28:7 says, "The Lord is my strength and my shield; in him my heart trusts, and I am helped; my heart exults, and with my song I give thanks to him." God wants to give you the power to live a life of joy, but it doesn't come by simply pulling up your boot straps or by *grinnin' and bearin'* it, nor by just gritting our teeth through it or by sucking it up and moving on in our own strength. No, joy only comes through God's power by prayer and the Holy Spirit. Let's pray for ourselves, but let's also pray for one another because it is through prayer that God's power is released in us.

We also find joy when we find hope in God. Let's look again at what Paul wrote in verses 19 to 20, "For I know that through your prayers and the help of the Spirit of Jesus Christ this will turn out for my deliverance, as it is my eager expectation and hope that I will not be at all ashamed, but that with full courage now as always Christ will be honored in my body, whether by life or by death." Paul really didn't know if he would live or die. He was in such a dire position that he didn't know if he would be released from prison or beheaded. I'm quite certain that if a lot of us were in the same situation as Paul, we would no doubt sink into a deep depression and maybe even get angry at God. So how did Paul live in such a state and still have joy in his life?

Note that he wrote in verse 20 that he lived in a state of hope and expectation. You see, he knew that one way or another he would be delivered. Either he would be set free in life, or he would be set free in death and live forever with Christ. He lived with the expectation of hope that everything would turn out for good. Hebrews 11:1 says, "Now faith is the assurance of things hoped for, the conviction of things not seen." Perhaps you have noticed that faith and hope go hand in hand. You cannot live a joyful life without hope. We need hope to cope. Our hope comes from being grounded in God's Word, which promises us a bright future regardless of what we are going through now.

There is one more essential ingredient needed to find joy. Joy comes when we discover God's purpose for our life. By the time the letter of Philippians was written, Paul was old and tired. He had been in prison for four years, and he was ready to go to heaven. His friends were free, but he was confined in prison. Others were out doing ministry, but his ministry has been limited to four walls. However, regardless of his circumstances, Paul was certain about his purpose in life. He wrote in verse 21, "For to me to live is Christ, and to die is gain." He wasn't saying that he wanted to die, but he was ready to die if that was God's plan for his life. However, while he was still living, his purpose in life was to serve Christ. There wasn't any other purpose that gave him greater joy than to be able to proclaim the love of Christ.

Let me ask you, how would you complete this sentence? "For me to live is [What?]." You may be saying to yourself, "I have no purpose. My life is meaningless." I would say to you that it is only meaningless if all you live for is possessions, pleasure, or power because there isn't any ultimate fulfillment in any of those things.

*****

*Barbara*

So as I ask myself this very question, "What am I living for?" I think back to the time before I married Mark and came across the verses in Matthew 16:24–25, "Then Jesus said to his disciples, 'If anyone would come after me, he must deny himself and take up his cross and follow me. For whoever wants to save his life will lose it, but whoever loses his life for me will find it.'" I didn't know what this might look like in the years to follow, but I knew that I desired to follow Christ. Not at the beginning, but maybe a significant decision in denying myself came when I knew that to become a mother, I needed to make a commitment to give up my career and be at home. That decision isn't required of everyone, but I felt that was what God was calling us to do as family. Mark and I felt committed to it. I had to reconcile my spiritual gifts in working in the financial industry and take a journey that would stretch me and grow me in ways I never imagined. Although I did not struggle with the decision, at times in the early days I did miss using my abilities and the challenges of my previous job.

Through the years, I have been encouraged with the words of Paul in Philippians, chapter 2, when he is telling us how we might go about denying ourselves. The word *denial* is not used, but there is no better example than that of Christ. Verses 5 to 8 state, "Your attitude should be the same as that of Christ Jesus: Who, being in very nature God, did not consider equality with God something to be grasped, but made himself nothing, taking the very nature of a servant, being made in human likeness. And being found in appearance as a man, he humbled himself and became obedient to death—even death on a cross!" It may be easy to read these words and to type these words in this moment, but to put these words into practice takes a day-by-day commitment to allow God to show us how to be a servant and the areas that we need to continue to allow Him access. And we need to be obedient in all things. That is what I have been striving after all these years in my own life.

*****

Why do I include this in a chapter on joy? Because through my life, and especially since the death of our son Nathan, I have found that by doing this, as my healing has continued (even though grief continues for our loss of Nathan), I have more joy and peace than I ever have known. Not because of what is visible, but because of the invisible, which is God's presence in my daily life. Perhaps the verses that start out chapter 2 in Philippians say it best: "If you have any encouragement from being united with Christ, if any comfort from his love, if any fellowship with the Spirit, if any tenderness and compassion, then make my joy complete by being like-minded, having the same love, being one in spirit and purpose." As much as God may give us people to bring blessing to our life, it has been through waiting on God and then seeing the truth of these verses playing out in my life that has brought me a level of joy and peace that I have never known.

Therefore, follow the example of Paul. He was looking at things in light of eternity. He knew what the future held because he knew the one who holds the future. Based on the example of Paul, the thing that can bring you the most joy in life is to invest your life in the next one. In fact, perhaps that can be your new purpose in life. Everyone will live for eternity, but where we spend it depends on where we invest our life. I suggest that you invest your life for Christ by putting your complete trust in Him, invite Him to be your Savior and Lord, and then begin serving Him. Your service does not save you. Only Jesus can do that. But your service will demonstrate that you are a child of God, and it will give you purpose in life. Only Christ can give you hope and purpose in life, and it is His hope that brings a joy-filled life.

God gave this poem to Barb. She is not normally a poet, but this came to her quickly and expresses the heart of a mother for her child.

It came on me quicker and sharper than birth pains.
It came from nowhere.
It came in the middle of celebration...150 years.
It came at the beginning of what could have been.
It came at the end of what was.
It was grief.
Grief unfathomable.

They told me I would find a new normal.
But what is normal?
Normal is a temperature of 98.6.
Normal is the heat of the summer and the cold of the winter.
Normal is a family of five, growing in numbers.
Normal is everyone having blue eyes (at
least if you're born a Barrett).

But...
Normal also means adjusting to what can never be again.
Normal is choosing every single day, as many times
as necessary, to trust in God and not myself.
Normal is allowing room for the continual pain, along
with the continual evidence of God's love.
Normal is not being afraid of tears when they show up unexpected.
Normal is not being ashamed of those same tears.

So many didn't show me, but thankfully Jesus did.
Jesus wept.
He wept even when He knew what was to come.

So I will follow Jesus's example. How can that not be normal?
I will weep and weep some more.
And I will rest in the truth that I, too,
Know what is to come.

Always in my heart, Nathan, always.
May 30, 1991–July 1, 2017

NATHAN
BARRETT

1991 - 2017

# ABOUT THE AUTHOR

Mark Barrett grew up in the State of Oregon. He has been a pastor for forty years ministering in eight churches in four Canadian provinces and two states. He received his education from Judson Baptist College, Moody Bible Institute, and Multnomah University. Mark has been married to Barbara for thirty-eight years. Together, they have three adult sons, two daughters-in-law, and four grandsons.

Ingram Content Group UK Ltd.
Milton Keynes UK
UKHW011831270423
420877UK00001B/61

REFERENCES

This paper is based primarily upon an analysis of the Aberdeen District Archives, Aberdeen Justice Court Book [AJCB], volumes I/2, II, and III, and Aberdeen Justice Court Accounts. The paper was read to a Scottish Records Association conference in Edinburgh on 26 October 1985.

1    Alexander Skene, *Memorials for the governments of the royal burghs in Scotland* (Aberdeen, 1685), 160.
2    AJCB, I/2, frontispiece.
3    For a list of most known sets of seventeenth century justice of the peace court records see B. Lenman, G. Parker, and P. Rayner, *Hand list of records for the study of crime in Early Modern Scotland* (List & Index Society, London, 1982), 71-5.
4    For further details see G.R. DesBrisay, Authority and discipline in Aberdeen, 1650-1700 (forthcoming thesis to be submitted to the University of St Andrews for the degree of Ph.D.).
5    *Acts of the parliaments of Scotland*, VI, ii, 833.
6    See, for example, Julia Buckroyd, 'Lord Broghill and the Scottish Church, 1655-1657', *Journal of Ecclesiastical History*, xxvii (1976), 359-68; F.D. Dow, *Cromwellian Scotland* (Edinburgh, 1979), 163-210; and L.M. Smith, Scotland and Cromwell: A study in Early Modern government (D.Phil. thesis, University of Oxford, 1979), 169-70.
7    *Selections from the ecclesiastical records of Aberdeen, 1562-1681*, ed. John Stuart (Spalding Club, 1846), 122.
8    On the number of English troops in Aberdeen, see DesBrisay, Authority and discipline; on the impact of the plagues see William Kennedy's unsurpassed *Annals of Aberdeen* (2 vols., Aberdeen, 1818), i, 271; while the influx of young Scots is based on an analysis of the Register of indentures of the Burgh of Aberdeen, A.M. Munro, *Scottish Notes and Queries*, x-xii (1897-8).
9    Kennedy, *Annals of Aberdeen*, i, 279.
10   Scottish Record Office, CH. 2/448/6, Aberdeen St Nicholas Kirk Session Minutes.
11   *Scottish Notes and Queries*, xiii (July 1898), 1-2.
12   See George B. Burnet, *The story of Quakerism in Scotland* (London, 1952), *passim*.
13   Skene, *Memorials*, 162. By the time this passage was published in 1685 Skene had been a Quaker for roughly fifteen years, and these views reflect the standard Quaker line on church-state relations as set out in 1678 by Robert Barclay, the Quaker apologist. According to Barclay's own testimony, *Apology* (1678), 251, however, Skene had

held these views long before becoming a Quaker. They presumably date from his brief fling with Independency in the early 1650s, and may therefore be taken as representative of his outlook at the time of the justice court's establishment in 1657.

14   Skene, *Memorials*, 162-3.

15   Ibid., 163.

16   Based on an analysis of lists of constables recorded each October, 1657-1700, in AJCB, I/2, II and III.

17   A copy of the constable's instructions is to be found in *Scottish Notes and Queries* (Nov. 1893), 87-8.

18   T.C. Smout, *A history of the Scottish people* (London, 1969), 159.

19   See DesBrisay, Authority and discipline.

20   The standard fine for fornication was £10, while a relapse paid £20, a trelapse £30, and so on. The fine for adultery was normally £40. Ante-nuptial fornication drew fines of anywhere from £3 for those who couldn't quite wait, to £9 for more blatant offenders. Scandalous carriage, too, could draw as little as £2, or as much as £10 for more serious peccadillos.

21   Most penalties for the various forms of disorderly conduct and Sabbath breach were in the 10/- to £3 range. In 1662 a man was fined only £1.10.0d for beating a fellow inhabitant on the head 'to the effusione of his blood', (AJCB, 1/2, f. 63). In seventeenth century Aberdeen a stray blow was seldom as costly as a surreptitious love affair.

22   Skene, *Memorials*, 164.

23   For a fuller description of these various developments, see DesBrisay, Authority and discipline.

24   Very few prosecutions for rape have come to light, and there are almost no hints of sexual assault in the Aberdeen records. It is quite conceivable, however, that violence was a factor in some of the sexual offences prosecuted by the justice court, though in how many or to what extent we shall probably never know.

25   B. Lenman and G. Parker, 'The state, the community, and the criminal Law in Early Modern Europe', in Lenman, Parker, and V.A.C. Gattrell, (eds.), *Crime and the Law: The social history of crime in Western Europe since 1500* (London, 1980), 23-46.

26   See DesBrisay, Authority and discipline, for more details.

27   Aberdeen Justice Court Accounts, 1679-80.

28   *Acts of the parliaments of Scotland*, VI, ii, 835; vii, 310.

29   AJCB, 1/2, f. 106.

30   AJCB, 1/2, f. 182.

31   AJCB, 1/2, f. 83.